STREETCARS and INTERURBANS of RICHLAND COUNTY, OHIO

VOLUME I
MANSFIELD-SHELBY-PLYMOUTH-NORWALK

BRETT DOUGLAS DUNBAR
With: Dennis Lamont and Brad Knapp

Published on Behalf of the Richland County Historical Society

Windjammer Adventure Publishing
Chagrin Falls, Ohio

Streetcars and Interurbans of Richland County, Ohio

©Copyright 2020 by Brett Douglas Dunbar

ISBN: 978-1-7333668-4-7

Library of Congress Control Number: 2020910624

All rights reserved under International and Pan-American Copyright Conventions. No part of this book may be reproduced or transmitted in any form without written permission of the author, except by reviewers who may use up to three images in connection with a review.

Windjammer Adventure P...
289 South Franklin Street, Chagrin ..., 44022
Telephone 440.247.6610 Email windjammerpub@mac.com

DEDICATION

This book is dedicated to the late Ron Simon of Mansfield. Ron was a life-long friend of mine and is most remembered for his wonderful articles in the Mansfield News Journal. While he wrote just about anything, nothing got him more excited or gave him more satisfaction than writing about history. Our common bond was our love specifically for transportation history. I miss his stories of when he was a child living in Shelby. On summer evenings he would bike out to Vernon Junction and chat with the tower operator. The crack passenger train #68, The Red Arrow, would blow by "about 8 o'clock" on the Pennsylvania Railroad, hammering the New York Central crossing at a terrific speed. Or the stories of watching the big T1's "smoke it up" out of Crestline while he sat at the Route 314 crossing – on his bike.

He served his country well. He fought in the Vietnam War and told miserable stories. But he was proud to have served his country and was a member of the American Legion.

Ron, my father, Jim, and I must have driven thousands of miles across the state of Ohio tracing rights-of-way of interurbans, streetcars, railroads, and canals. Exploring was the fun part for my father and me, but Ron had writing to do when he got home. Sure enough, on Sunday morning a big article about the previous day's trip would be in his section, "Stuff," in the Mansfield News Journal. I'm sure he didn't go to bed Saturday night until that article was written and submitted!

Ron also loved books. When we would get together, the first hour or so was spent discussing which books he had finally "picked up" or which ones he still really wanted. He loved books so much it really became just about buying and collecting. One time he bought so many history books in one week he admitted he knew he'd never have time to read them. But he was glad he had bought them.

Although this book will never be enough to give credit for the inspiration that Ron gave me, it is fitting. He loved history. He loved books. What better way for me to show my appreciation to him than dedicating my first history book to him? At one time he joked that if I ever got around to writing one, that he'd at least "rate a footnote in it." Well, Ron, you get far more than a footnote. This book strives to encompass some of the things you loved. And you get a dedication.

I'll leave a copy for you at the top of Mt. Jeez.

INTRODUCTION

Streetcars and Interurbans of Richland County, Ohio, Volume I, covers a portion of transportation history in Richland County and northern Ohio. This work aims to provide a relatively complete history of two interurban lines and what was referred to as a "paper railroad." These routes are historically significant to the county and northern Ohio because they played a major role in influencing the way transportation changed over time. Some of these routes have personal meaning to many residents as well as past family members. Many residents have shared memories of riding on, observing, or working on one of the systems.

To understand what an interurban was, one must understand a streetcar system. Streetcars were a popular mode of transportation within cities beginning in the late 1800s lasting into the 1950s. They made their appearance when streets were unpaved and there were no automobiles. Northern Ohio winters were cold and streetcars offered a means for warmer travel. Powered by overhead electric current, they were considered a "clean" mode of transportation. Streetcar systems operated only within their city limits.

What was an interurban? An interurban could be thought of in simple terms as a streetcar system that left city limits and ventured out into the countryside to reach other urban areas. When interurbans were first put into use there were no automobiles. Roads for horse-and-buggy were too muddy and unimproved, and riding the railroad was dirty and sooty due to the big steam engines. Canals were painfully slow. The interurban offered a unique mode of transportation: Everyday people could hop on the car and ride to wherever they wanted to go. Service was frequent, convenient and cheap—there was no need to wait around 2 hours or buy an expensive ticket. One could walk to the corner to the waiting room and usually, within 15 to 30 minutes, a car would come by. High school sports teams would travel by interurban much like today they travel by bus. Unfortunately for the interurban, roads did improve—and Henry Ford was able to develop a mass-produced automobile at an affordable price beginning in 1908. After that, ridership on streetcars and interurbans began a severe decline. Some folded as early as the 1920s, and only the most successful lasted into the 1930s. Interurbans, therefore, can be thought of as a "bridging" mode of transportation between horse-and-buggy days to the days of fast automobiles, and was certainly one of the shortest-lived modes of transportation in U.S. history.

Lastly, many "paper railroads" were constructed in Ohio. Paper railroads were just like the name implies – on paper only. Promotors, to drum up investor money, would incorporate railroad companies and plan routes but never actually build a grade and lay ties and rails, much less operate a real railroad. Richland County had a unique situation. A con man decided to construct a railroad that at first glance seemed to be on pace to be on paper only. In this case, however, the grade was constructed and all approaches and fills to bridges were completed. Unfortunately, only a very small section of rail was laid.

This volume is divided into four parts. *Part I* describes the Mansfield & Shelby Electric Railway Company, a very popular interurban line that ran from Mansfield to Shelby, with a brief overview of the Mansfield city streetcar system. *Part II* describes the Sandusky, Norwalk, and Mansfield Electric Railway, an interurban line that operated from Norwalk south to Shelby with an extension over to Chicago Junction (later Willard). *Part III* describes an ill-fated company that took over the SN&M after it had been abandoned, known as the Norwalk and Shelby Railroad. Lastly, *Part IV* is a history of the famous con man Charles French and his network of railroads, some real and some not, in Richland County.

The first day of operations of the streetcar system in Mansfield open to the public was August 8, 1887. Here is Mansfield Electric Street Railway car #1 at the corner of North Main Street and North Park Street, posing for a photo. (Timothy Brian McKee)

PART I
THE MANSFIELD & SHELBY ELECTRIC RAILWAY COMPANY

The Mansfield & Shelby Electric Railway was a popularized interurban line that ran from Mansfield to Shelby from June of 1901 to the end of February 1934. It was one of the longest-lasting interurbans in the country and was also one of the true interurbans by definition in the country. It was owned by the Mansfield streetcar system its entire life and so was truly an extension of a streetcar system out into the countryside to reach another municipality. For just under 33 years, citizens of Mansfield could ride to Shelby to meet crack Big Four passenger trains, or later when the Sandusky, Norwalk, and Mansfield Electric Railway reached Shelby, could take a ride to Sandusky and Cedar Point. Likewise, Shelby citizens could ride over to Mansfield perhaps for an afternoon at Luna or Casino Parks or meet a Cleveland Southwestern interurban to go over to Seccaium Park between Galion and Bucyrus. The M&S was the first interurban to operate in Richland County, Ohio. It is hoped the reader will enjoy the history, photos, and memories of the route.

The Beginning - The Mansfield Electric Street Railway Company

The M&S interurban line owes its existence to the Mansfield streetcar system at the time, the Mansfield Electric Street Railway Company. It was a direct extension of that city system to Shelby and was classified as a "true interurban" or suburban line. It began back on March 30, 1887, the day that Mansfield City Council granted a franchise to S. T. Dunham of New York to construct and operate a city streetcar system that would use overhead "trolley wheel" power. At about the same time the ordinance was granted, the Mansfield Electric Street Railway Company was incorporated by Mr. Van Rensselaer, *et. al.,* with a capital stock of $75,000. Later, officers were named as follows: Ed Oothout, president; C. E. McBride, secretary; M. Van Rensselaer Jr., treasurer; W. G. Root, manager; and John F. Gay, assistant manager. The promoters wanted to have the line open for the big July 4 celebration. It didn't happen. Because of a slew of operational problems with equipment, the opening day kept getting delayed. The big day finally came on August 8, 1887, which was the first official day open to the public (even though test running had been done the previous two days with no problems). At best estimates, this would make it the 4th streetcar system to open in the country and the 2nd in Ohio (behind Lima). At first the lines were woefully incomplete; there was a very basic operating route and it took quite some time to get all of the routes built, developed, and operational. But it was a start.

The Mansfield Herald – She's a Go – First Trial Trip

Prior to the opening day, however, there had been a trial run on the streetcar system. This took place on Wednesday, August 3, 1887 using car #1. The real opening event occurred later on Monday, August 8, 1887. Both accounts were recorded in detail by the Mansfield Herald and must be included here as these accounts truly take the reader back in time and one can almost feel as though they are present for each event. The station was at today's 6th & Main.

August 3, 1887: A Herald reporter was given a quiet tip early Tuesday evening (August 2) that car No. 1 would be given a trial trip, as a test, between twelve and one o'clock (August 3).

Midnight found the reporter at the central station. On going down a couple of men were attaching a wire to the overhead conducting wire.

At the station the employees, Superintendent Root, Inspector Gay, Engineer Neftel, Messrs. Squires and Lloyd, President Huntington Brown, and Mr. J. E. Brown were found.

Steam was up and Messrs. Neftel, Squires and Lloyd were at work over the dynamo.

At 12:50 everything was in readiness; the wire connected and the engine started. In the meantime car No. 1 was run out by hand to the front of the Laver block.

The "trolley," a device that runs along the over-head wires, from which the wire that conducts the electric current to the motor, was placed in a position and at just 1 o'clock the current was turned on. The power at this time was 230 volts.

At least one hundred people surrounded the car as the three incandescent lamps shed their soft light through the car, which was a beautiful sight to behold.

Number One was in the charge of Superintendent Root, with Mr. Squires at the lever. The word to start was given and the car moved off at a good rate of speed. It moved along smoothly, with but very little noise and without a hitch. The car was not put to its greatest speed. The corner of Bloom Street was reached in less than two minutes. Then came the climb up the steep Main Street grade. The hill was mounted in good shape, and much faster than four horses could pull the car.

The corner of Fourth Street was reached in just two minutes. Here a stop of a few minutes was made to examine the machinery. All was found right and the cars started back. When the car reached the brow of the hill, she was let go and a glorious coast down the hill was had. The car fairly flew, and it took just thirty seconds to get to the foot.

In the car and on the rear platform were about thirty people. Among those that enjoyed the first ride of the street car were the officers above mentioned, Mr. J. E. Brown, Capt. A. C. Cummins, M. Rumbaugh, the Cincinnati architect; Riley Bange, George Forney, John Murphy, Walter Grubaugh, O. P. Reed, Geo. A. McCracken, E. P. Hawley and Officer Underwood.

When the car was started there was a scramble to put the fare, a nickel, into the box. John Murphy got there first, and for years to come, he can tell how his nickel was the first put into the fair box for a ride.

The Mansfield Herald Reports, Day 1

August 9, 1887: "You can rely on it; we will make a trial trip Monday morning." That is what Engineer Neftel said to a Herald reporter Sunday evening.

Early Monday morning all hands were at work and at about 9 o'clock car No. 1 was run out of the station. A larger crowd soon gathered and in a few minutes the attachments were made and the officers and a few invited guests got aboard. Several runs were made back and forth to Bloom Street. Everything worked to a charm and at about 10 o'clock the car was started up the hill. With only about 75 percent of the power on, the car ran up the hill in fine style. The time consumed in going from Bloom Street to the European Hotel was just one minute and forty seconds.

A great crowd lined both sides of the street as the car glided along smoothly and almost noiselessly to Market Street. When she turned the curve not a jar was felt. As the "trolley" was passing the insulator on the curve it stuck fast and the brass spring broke. This was altogether due to the overhead wire being a little out of line and a defect that was easily remedied.

A few minutes later the car was again started and in just four minutes it reached Senator Sherman's residence. Returning, the car fairly flew over the ground, making excellent time.

A test of the brake was made on the steepest part of the Main Street hill. The car was brought to a standstill instantly and the speed going down the hill was increased or decreased at will.

There has been a number of objections made that the car would frighten horses. No fewer that one hundred horses, driven to all sorts of vehicles, were passed on the round trip and only two of the number showed fright.

Campbell and Seiler, the photographers, took negatives of the car, the former in front of the establish-

ment and the latter at the station with the officers and employees surrounding the car.

The Daft System: *Six years ago there was not a single electric railway in the world. Two years ago there was not one doing a regular business, today there are upwards of a dozen in operation and many more in the various stages of organization and construction. Among the first to realize the great future for electric power in America was Mr. Leo Daft, who for the last six or seven years has devoted his time and energy to the study and practical development of electric motors for propulsion of cars and stationary work.*

The car which surprised many spectators yesterday with the ease with which it climbed Main Street hill, is one of the results of his ingenuity.

There are many systems of electric propulsion both in operation and on paper, but the Daft system has many.

Features peculiar to itself which commend it to capitalists interested in street railway enterprises.

You have noticed that the motor is under the car, supported directly by the axles to which it is geared with accurately cut steel gearing. No chains nor belts are used. The cars can be run equally well from either and easily reversed.

There is no fear of watches being magnetized, as the motor is protected by a magnetic shield.

The cars are lit by three incandescent lamps which make it possible to read a newspaper in any part of the car.

The Daft company have experimented in all kinds of railroading with electricity and use methods to suit local conditions. They are running on the Ninth Avenue Elevated railroad in New York; have a road in Baltimore, where the current is carried by the rails and two roads in Los Angeles, California, using overhead conductors stretched on poles having arms.

They are building roads at Ashbury Park, N. J., Ithaca, N. Y., and Middletown, Conn., with wires like those in Mansfield, but using iron poles.

In Pittsburgh they are constructing a road with grades just twice as steep as the steepest on the Mansfield road and carrying the current into the city under ground in a sort of drain between the rails which is reached by a brush going down through a narrow slot in an iron conduit.

Power Distribution: *The company has also given its attention to the distribution of power and their stationary motors are in use in many cities. Down in a subcellar in New York a nest of engines and dynamos are humming and thundering all day long, year in and year out, while many manufacturers are running machinery in the top floors of distant buildings with the electricity supplied to them through insignificant looking wires stretched around alleys and house tops. Elevators, printing presses, fans and whole shops are thus run by Daft motors, and the consumers of power never have to look at the machine, the only attention required by the motor being a daily visit by a small boy from the central power station with an oil can.*

There are a thousand and one things which people naturally want to know about electric street cars and electricity itself. They can understand more about it in five minutes when they see the thing going than by ten years of explanation before it starts. The company therefore being weary of trying to explain to people and giving free lectures to their friends have concluded to set the thing going and let people see for themselves.

It is rumored that the Mansfield Electric Street Railway Company expect to furnish power to small consumers by means of these stationary motors.

The Current Not Dangerous: *One of the principle characteristics of the Daft system is the low tension of the current used. If a man took hold of the wires of any other electric railway system he would die instantly, whereas the Daft wires would only shake him up a little. It is not advisable for small boys to monkey with the wires and the company will not be held responsible for accidents which might thereby occur, but it is some satisfaction to know that people can come in contact with the wires and not suffer seriously in consequence. As for the cars themselves, they are much better protected from accident than a steamboat is from explosion or an ordinary carriage from the tricks of a horse.*

The Trip Last Night: If the crowd on the streets was large yesterday, it was monstrous last night, especially in the vicinity of the turn at Market and Main Streets.

The car moved out of central station at exactly 7:55 last evening loaded to its utmost with the city council and invited guests to the number of thirty-one. It ran along smoothly to the foot of the hill when, the track being wet, it stuck for a moment, but soon caught the rail with the aid of sand and ran O. K. until the end of the line at Senator Sherman's residence.

A large crowd had assembled at the corner of Main and Market Streets to see the trolley go around the curve which it did very nicely, no doubt agreeably surprising a great many. On the return trip Mr. Knight Neftel announced to the council that they would stop at a restaurant and partake in a fine lunch.

Cars To Run Regularly Today: Mr. Neftel wishes us to announce that this one car will commence running regularly today and will make as many trips as possible. No schedule in regard to running time will be made as yet, but as soon as the other cars are equipped, which will be in a few days, a regular schedule will be made.

On Wednesday night the car will run continually on Market Street from Main to accommodate those who wish to attend the festival given by the St. Luke's Lutheran Church on the lawn of Mr. M. D. Harter.

The Lunch: After the car was run into the station last night, by invitation of the company, the city council, ex-councilman and a few other gentlemen congregated at an up-town restaurant for lunch, Messrs. Dunham, Lloyd, Neftel, Root, Gay, Brown, and McBride of the company, were present. Each person present responded to toasts and Mr. Neftel spoke at length. He said that the company had already spent $72,000 in the plant and that it had abundant capital at its back to push the line to the park, Intermediate prison, and up Marion Avenue and elsewhere and would do so when there was a demand for car service to those places.

At present the four and a half miles would be all that would be operated. He declared that no horse car company could operate in this city with financial success on account of the hills; that such a company would require from forty to fifty horses, and besides this, the streets would need to be repaired at least twice a year. With the electric system no fire trap barns are required, no streets to repair and the track will last upwards of ten years without repair. He stated as his opinion that the line in this city was better built and equipped than any other line in the country, and that it most certainly would be inspected by every company who proposed to build a street railway line.

Every one present spoke well of the manner in which the line was constructed.

The party adjourned at 1 o'clock this morning in an amiable frame of mind.

If travel on the West Market Street cars increases it will be necessary to add to the capacity of the line and this fact reminds me of an article in the September Harper on street railways in South America. There the cars are rendered quite picturesque and their capacity increased by an arrangement for carrying passengers on the top of the car, which is reached by stairways on either side of the rear entrance.

Another pleasing feature is the neat figure of the lady conductress who has her position between the stairways and receives the tickets before the passengers enter the car.

Eventually lines were extended outward from the original main core from the "central station" at North Main and West Sixth to various locations, such as the fairgrounds at Springmill and Burns. Here is car #5 southbound on Springmill Street at Prescott, in 1887, on an early run. The overhead wiring and power system as shown above was known as the Daft System and employed 4 overhead trolley wheels that sat on top of two wires – a negative and a positive. This would last until 1891, when the Sprague System, with a single overhead wire and trolley wheel, was employed. The home in the background was recently demolished (2019). (Timothy Brian McKee)

> *Arrayed in her white apron with its many pockets for the reception of tickets, change, etc., she adds much to the picturesqueness of the picture given.*
>
> *The cool nights and comfortable days indicate the near autumn time, fairest and saddest season of the year. Its red leaves and fair flowers are things of beauty, and its cool sunny days and balmy air a delight, but they are laden with the presage of death to foliage and flower, and precursors of the bitter winter, cold, and storm.*

Operations eventually branched out to South Park, the Casino, the fairgrounds, Union Depot, and the cemetery. The Reformatory Line wasn't completed until late 1892, with operations beginning in the spring of 1893. The line at first operated with what was called the Daft System as mentioned in the Herald account. The Daft System employed 4 trolley wheels in a square orientation that sat up on top of two overhead wires. The single wheel system that is so familiar wasn't adopted until 1891, known as the Sprague System, and used a single wire.

Many, many interurban and streetcar parts were manufactured by the Ohio Brass Company in Mansfield. These included, but were not limited to, overhead wire, cross arms, bars, motor parts, wire guards, etc.

Citizen's Electric Railway, Light & Power Company

On April 10, 1891, the Citizen's Electric Railway, Light & Power Company was incorporated in New

CERL&P Co. car #2 is seen southbound on Springmill Street sometime later after the Sprague System had been employed (single overhead wire and trolley wheel). This car seems to be either coming or going to a baseball game. Mansfielders for years used the streetcar system to travel just about anywhere because there were no automobiles yet and horse and buggy was either slower or colder than the novel streetcar. (Timothy Brian McKee)

York with a capital stock of $125,000. The head capitalist was a Mr. Clark Rude. Also in 1891, that company took over the Mansfield Electric Street Railway; now known as the Citizen's Electric Railway, Light & Power Company, many improvements were planned and implemented. For example, the system was completely operational, after 1895, to the fairgrounds, cemetery, Sherman-Heineman Park (both South Park and North Lake Park/Casino), Union Depot, and the Reformatory. Shortly after the "take-over" by the CERL&P Company, two prominent Mansfield businessmen, S. N. Ford and Reid Carpenter, purchased the company for themselves (12/1892). Other officers associated with them were M. D. Harter and Rush Taggert. And it is here where the Mansfield-Shelby interurban line gets its roots.

Carpenter and Ford were sensitive to the way Mansfield businessmen felt about the NYC Big Four route supposedly "snubbing" Mansfield and building their mainline to the west through Shelby and Crestline. It was incredibly difficult and inconvenient for citizens to reach Cleveland for instance. One solution would be to build an interurban line from Mansfield to Shelby where the Big 4 RR could be reached and that is ultimately what ended up happening.

Plans for the interurban line began as early as 1896. Shelby City Council held a meeting as early as February 3, 1897, to hear and grant the CERL&P a franchise to construct the line within Shelby city limits. The route at that time, however, was completely different than the one that was actually built later. On December 15, 1897, the county franchise from the Richland County commissioners was granted, but again, a different route was finally built. It wasn't until March 21, 1898, that a meeting of the stockholders of the CERL&P met and unanimously passed the monetary amounts to be used for reconstructing and improving their physical plant; $175,000 was allotted to be used for the construction of the interurban line to Shelby. The bonds were payable to the Cleveland Trust Company. It was quite a while before actual ordinances were issued for the construction. The route through Mansfield was designated as north on Bowman Street to where said street crosses the Pennsylvania Railroad. At that point the line would follow the south edge of the Pennsylvania Railroad to a point just west of Leppo Road on the Twitchell Farm, where it would then go over the railroad on a combination steel and wooden bridge. From there the line would follow the west side of the B&O Railroad to Shelby. Shelby's route was also changed from the original franchise. After following the west side of the B&O, the line would turn due west in the middle of Tucker Avenue in Shelby. Next it would turn north on Mack Avenue and turn due west on Park to reach the Black Fork. From there the line was to follow the east side of the Black Fork to the corner of East Main Street and Mohican Street. The original franchise had the line running north up Mohican and straight across East Smiley to the Big Four depot. However, the land was too marshy and low for Reid Carpenter so the franchise was modified a second time to turn due east onto East Smiley and then turn north along the B&O RR to reach the Big Four depot on higher ground.

Things weren't always easy in Shelby. City Council had mixed feelings about the interurban coming to town. Lot 582, a lot between the old fire house and the Black Fork at Main Street, caused some serious problems for Reid Carpenter & Company. On October 11, 1900, councilman Anderson of Shelby claimed that a local citizen had offered $1500 for that small lot and that there was no reason Reid Carpenter shouldn't pay at least that, or else the citizen had the right to the lot (the citizen was V. O. Peters). Apparently this angered Carpenter and the local newspaper said he was made to look 10 years older. After an ensuing argument and rather lengthy meeting, council was adjourned. An agreement was finally made at a later meeting on November 22, 1900. Reid Carpenter and his interurban line would lease the lot for 25 years at $1250. The remaining strip of school grounds that the school board owned south along the Black Fork was also leased at $500, and the track had to stay "as near the Black Fork as possible" so as not to use anymore of the school's grounds than necessary. This lease was perpetual. On November 25, 1900, since the franchise had been altered to run on higher ground along the B&O up to the Shelby depot as previously mentioned, it was agreed that a new street would be constructed at this point (later to become Mohican Street Extension) and that the interurban would pay 1/3 of the total cost. The final and full official ordinance in Shelby was granted December 21, 1900.

With all franchises and ordinances approved, it was time to begin construction of the line. Construction went very quickly due to the fact that the line was only 12 miles long. The only significant obstacle was the overpass at Spring Mill over the Pennsylvania Railroad. Prior to grading, the CERL&P did two other important upgrades. They added machinery to their powerhouse on the northwest corner of North Main Street and West Sixth Street in Mansfield, and they expanded the car barn capacity at the car barns at East Fourth Street and Scott Street. It should be mentioned, however, that the Mansfield franchise and ordinance had been approved long before the Shelby situation. In fact that franchise was still good from the 1897-1898 era and so approximately in July of 1900, prior to the Shelby incidences, work began up Bowman Street. In September of 1900, the line was finished to a point known as Terman Hill near where Bowman Street had crossed the Pennsylvania Railroad. On Monday September 24, 1900, the first run was up to Terman Hill by streetcar #11. It was ridden only by the workmen constructing the line but it was good progress and good news to the citizens.

By November 15, 1900, the expanded car barns had been completed and on December 31, 1900, the

In 1900, the Citizen's Electric Railway, Light & Power Company moved their original car barns from the northwest corner of North Main Street and West Sixth Street, to the southwest corner of East Fourth Street and Scott Street. The old car barns were outdated and dilapidated. The new car barns would be much larger and could house more cars. The main motivation behind such a move was the coming of the Mansfield-Shelby interurban line. The big new interurban cars would require a larger storage space. In addition, the powerhouse was expanded due to a higher demand in electricity for the interurban. The removal of the car barn at the powerhouse site allowed more space for the addition to the powerhouse. (Timothy Brian McKee)

power house upgrades had also been completed. Work progressed steadily over the next few months, stopping only for inclement winter weather. Rails and grading were completed on both sides of the Spring Mill bridge over the PRR. The fill along with the bridge would be 722 ft. long total. On February 8, 1901, the final touches were put on the bridge and all that had to be done was to connect the rail at each end. A second power line was being sent out of the power house from Mansfield to this bridge to act as a "booster" to make sure sufficient power was being sent to the interurban cars for two reasons: to enable the cars to make the full trip to Shelby on enough power and to ensure that the cars could make the steep climb up the bridge. The second wire tied into the main overhead wire at a point just beyond the bridge. As a result, on March 21, 1901, special poles to handle this rather complicated arrangement of wires were installed. This will be explained later. By May 24, the track gang reached the Globe Works at Shelby but had to wait on a grading modification along the high school. The bridge that would go over the stream south of Main Street would need to be 18 inches higher than the grading had been done. Also in May, the CERL&P ordered their interurban cars to be used on the Mansfield-Shelby line. They were ordered from the G. C. Kuhlman Car Company in Cleveland,

Ohio. They were to be made of fine wood, painted dark red, and would be 41 ½ feet long. The motors would allow for operation from both ends of the car so the cars would not have to back up to return to either Shelby or Mansfield. The motorman could simply walk to the other end of the car, change the controller and head back. The cars were numbered 40, 42, and 44. At this time it should be mentioned that a new generator was added to the powerhouse, a second improvement.

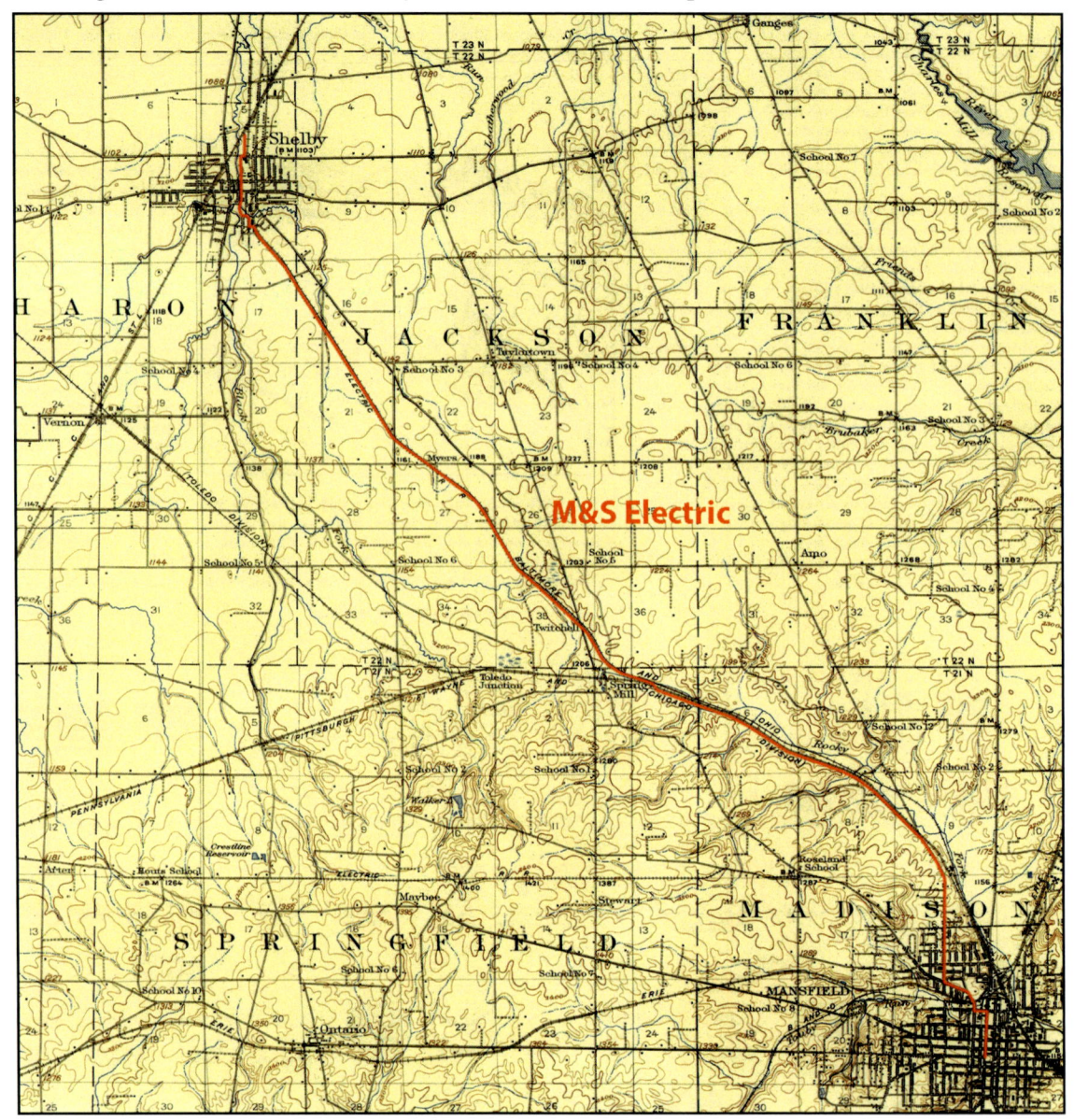

The M&S line was constructed from Mansfield to Shelby as shown above in the USGS Crestline Quadrangle map from 1915. (Courtesy of the USGS)

Although the line hadn't opened yet, on June 13, 1901, a lot of information was released by the company regarding operations. An operating schedule that would become effective July 1 was issued. The ticket offices were listed at the company offices which were at the powerhouse at the time, as well as Harland Walter's Cigar Store and C. S. Ashbrook's Drug Store, all in Mansfield. There was no ticket office established in Shelby yet. Two cars would leave every hour, one departing each from Mansfield and Shelby. The first car would leave Mansfield public square at 5:15 AM with the second one leaving at 6:00 AM. Cars would then leave hourly until 10:00 PM. On the Shelby end, cars were scheduled to leave Shelby Junction out at the Big Four depot at 6:00 AM and every hour after that until 10:00 PM. The fare was 25 cents one way or 45 cents round trip. Individual fares were from

Mansfield and listed as 5 cents to Siding 1 on Bowman Street, 10 cents to Twitchell's Road (later Leppo Road), 15 cents to Myer's Road, and 20 cents to Siding 3 (outside of Shelby). To be complete, it should be mentioned that Siding 2 was near the Spring Mill overpass. The line was 12 miles long and contained 22 stops. Schedules allowed for a 36 minute run time.

Finally, on Wednesday afternoon June 19, 1901, a trial trip was made from Mansfield to Shelby on car #44. On the trip were Reid Carpenter, S. N. Ford, Superintendent A. J. Haycox, Mrs. Haycox and children, Frank Fast, Charles L. Slough, W. A. Duff, Edward Moser, Meade Cunningham, and motorman William Peterson. The ticket office and waiting room in Shelby was established at the northwest corner of Main Street and Mohican Street.

The big day came on Thursday, June 20, 1901, when the line was opened to the public. Car #44 left Mansfield for Shelby on the first official public run and operated on a "two-hourly" schedule. The first car left Mansfield at 2:00 PM and ran to Main Street in Shelby. It returned from Shelby and then left Mansfield again at 4:00 PM, thus the term "two-hourly" schedule. The crew on the new line were motormen Rufus Hale, Ben Wigton, and Frank Sipe. The conductors were Tom Williams, Willard Mitchell, and Bert Keckler. A motorman and conductor were assigned to each of the 3 cars – 40, 42, and 44. At first, the line wasn't constructed very well according to records. In fact, even as late as 1908 (as will be seen) the SN&M did not feel comfortable with operating their cars to Mansfield over the M&S tracks because the management didn't feel the right-of-way could sustain the weight of the SN&M's big combination passenger/freight cars. The ticket office and waiting room in Shelby were in the building on the northwest corner of Main and Mohican. The building was owned by Mr. and Mrs. Joseph Hodges. There was a Western Union office there too and Mrs. Effie Hodges, the wife, was the agent for both the interurban and Western Union.

The next day, on June 21, 1901, the interurban began its first full day of the hourly schedule. Cars left Mansfield at 5:30 AM that day and ran hourly to Shelby and back. The last car left Shelby for Mansfield at 10:00 PM. The interurban was heavily patronized that day due to the Republican Convention in Mansfield. The only fault in the operations was the fact that the line didn't go north of Main Street in Shelby yet. The schedule read a time at the Shelby Junction location, but no track was even constructed out there yet. It was a problem the CERL&P took at least another 2 months to overcome. Sensitive to this issue the CERL&P did hire Mr. Weddell, the city engineer of Shelby, to survey that route out to Shelby Junction on June 21. Meanwhile the line was well-patronized and there was even some excitement near Spring Mill along the B&O. The new interurban cars had incredibly bright headlights, not to mention the fact that few citizens were used to seeing these cars running. Included in that group of people not used to the cars and the headlights were B&O railroad crews. As mentioned the lines paralleled one another from Spring Mill to Shelby. On the night of June 26, 1901, a B&O freight train running from Chicago Junction to Mansfield was approaching Spring Mill. On the interurban line a northbound car for Shelby, in the charge of motorman Frank Sipes, came around the curve just north of Spring Mill. When the B&O crew saw the big headlight, instead of thinking it was an interurban car, they thought it was another B&O train on the same track about to collide head-on with them! As a result the engineer and fireman jumped for their lives out of the locomotive just as the interurban car casually passed by on the interurban track.

On August 23, 1901, the overhead trolley wire was strung from Main Street in Shelby, north to the Shelby Big 4 depot, to Shelby Junction. Streetcars and interurbans typically built the grade and laid the ties and rails prior to stringing wire, but this oddly was not the case. However, it was only 4 days later on August 27, 1901, that the track gang got busy and began building the line out to the junction. It was finished shortly thereafter. The schedule always started with Shelby Junction (not

Shelby) and so it was a very big relief for the company to get this section operating. Next, on October 18, a fence was built along the right-of-way next to Shelby High School for safety purposes.

> **MANSFIELD & SHELBY INTER-URBAN RAILWAY.**
> RUNNING TIME 36 MINUTES.
> Leave Mansfield 5:27 a. m., 5:57 a. m. and hourly thereafter until and including 6:57 p. m.; then 8:57 p. m. and 10:57 p. m.
> Leave Shelby 6:10 a. m., 7:05 a. m. and hourly thereafter until and including 8:05 p. m., then 10:05 and 11:45 p. m.
> Sundays—First car leaves Mansfield at 5:57 a. m., and Shelby 7:00 a. m.

A Brief Mention of the Power

The CERL&P had a powerhouse on the northwest corner of North Main Street and West Sixth Street in Mansfield. It was a primitive setup as DC electricity was sent out into what was called a feeder wire. Every 1000 feet the feeder wire would "feed" into the trolley wire which was used to power the motors. Unique to the M&S in those early days was the stringing of a second feeder wire from the powerhouse out to the Pennsylvania Railroad overpass at Spring Mill. This second wire was fed by a "booster" in the powerhouse. It didn't tie into the overhead trolley wire until a point just beyond the PRR bridge. This booster gave additional power to cars running to Shelby and also helped cars climb the steep grade over the PRR. The typical operating voltage in the overhead trolley wire was 600V DC. At this time the powerhouse site was also where the main waiting room and office were located for the streetcar and interurban, but the old car barns which were originally located there were closed and new ones were built on East Fourth Street at Scott Street in 1900.

The streetcar system and the interurban line to Shelby were powered by a powerhouse located on the northwest corner of North Main Street and West Sixth Street. Shown here is a postcard view of some of the interior – dynamos and rotary converters. The main generator is located behind the photographer. This powerhouse was effective from 1887 to 1917 at which time the big MELCO plant southeast of Lucas was turned to "full blast." There were two flywheel explosions during its lifetime: 1906 and 1916. In 1919 it burned to the ground by a fire of unknown origin. The powerhouse had been upgraded several times over the years and generated power as mentioned for the streetcars and interurban, but also for sale commercially. (Timothy Brian McKee)

> ## "A Thing of Beauty is a Joy Forever"
>
> 42   M & S.   42
>
> G.C. KUHLMAN CAR CO.
> BUILDERS CLEVELAND, O.
>
> Designers and Builders of all classes of City and Suburban Cars.
> For Comfort, Beauty, Strength and Durability, we excel.

G. C. Kuhlman builder's illustration of the Mansfield-Shelby interurban line car #42 (Cleveland State Collection)

The Early Operations

On the first day the line began operating under a separate name called the Mansfield & Shelby Electric Railway. The early operations are fairly well-known but what is not fully understood is the early equipment. Since the CERL&P was really the streetcar company in Mansfield several cars were mixed in or substituted in and out with regular cars 40, 42, and 44. For example, in 1901, the city system already was running a summer "open car" between Mansfield and Shelby occasionally to help the other 3 regular cars with days of excessive business. A second open car was built specifically for the intermittent use on the interurban line in early 1902, and so the streetcar company had two of them to run in the summers in the first few years of the interurban. The second one was a very good car. It was 43 feet long, had 15 seats, and would easily seat about 75 people—if cramming were required, perhaps 100 could be seated. Also of note was the fact that the interurban line began serving its larger purpose in March of 1902. The Big Four train #26, beginning March 20, 1902, would wait 30 minutes longer at the Shelby Big Four depot for the 6:00 AM interurban car out of Mansfield. This was done specifically for passengers wishing to travel from Mansfield to Cleveland. It was a very popular run because Mansfielders for the first time had a quick route to Cleveland!

Not only did the interurban line carry passengers, it also carried freight. On September 4, 1902, an express package and freight service was begun on the Mansfield-Shelby interurban line. A separate freight car was constructed and put into operation that carried only freight and no passengers. The M&S freight car was very primitive. According to the *Street Railway Journal,* instead of buying a dedicated "freight motor" they decided to build their own and use that until at least the proposition proved profitable. A large double-truck, open passenger car not suitable for interurban use was chosen. The seats were removed and the sides covered in wooden sheaths or "matched" siding. Large double-doors were cut on the sides to load in freight. The car was fitted with four 35-HP (horsepower) motors and air brakes and by 1904 was making two round trips between Mansfield and Shelby. The cost back then was "7 cents per cwt" or 7 cents per centum weight. A centum weight in the United States meant 100 pounds. Originally, the car made only one round trip and left Mansfield at 9:30 AM and arrived in Shelby at 10:15 AM. After 2 weeks that schedule was adjusted to one hour later. During that time extra runs could be done due to the Central Fruit Company chartering the car on occasion. Freight points were at Shelby, 4th and Main, and the square.

In 1903, some changes occurred to both the interurban line and the streetcar line from an administrative viewpoint. The first item was the election of officers for the CERL&P on January 21, 1903. S. N. Ford was elected president; C. F. Ackerman, vice president; S. G. Cummings, secretary; and Reid Carpenter, treasurer. Meanwhile another organization was being formed "behind the scenes" in Cincinnati. The capital stock of the CERL&P was increased from $400,000 to $1,000,000. On March 19, 1903, it became clear why. The company formed was called the Mansfield Railway, Light & Power Company. The franchise and stock were transferred on this day from the CERL&P to the MRL&P. Some changes occurred on the board of directors and officers. S. N. Ford was removed as president and replaced by the Cincinnati interests who picked H. M. Byllesby of Chicago; he represented the Cincinnati trust firm of Rudolph Kleybolte & Company. Sidney A. Foltz was elected general manager shortly thereafter. While nothing else negative happened to the streetcar or interurban, people were at first worried. However, the MRL&P ended up being a big blessing to the system as nothing but great improvements occurred during those years. For instance there were several power upgrades and the line from Mansfield to Shelby was rebuilt in part and re-ballasted the entire way. Many bridges and culverts were also redone to higher standards and most of them were done entirely in steel and concrete. The 3 cars were also all equipped with air brakes. On May 28, 1903, the two open summer cars were also placed into service on the Shelby line in order to alleviate crowds.

On March 9, 1905, the streetcar system and the interurban line got a new ticket office and waiting room in Mansfield. The old office was in relatively poor condition being located next to the powerhouse and old car barns at 251 North Main Street. On this day they moved to 3 North Main Street in the Brucker and Barbour Building. The Ohio Central Traction Company operated an interurban line from Mansfield to Bucyrus and had its own ticket office and waiting room at 7 North Main Street in Ozier's Cigar Store. Other improvements included the repair, refitting, and repainting of car #40. On July 21, 1905, it was released from the streetcar shops at the car barns on East Fourth Street greatly improved and ready for hard service.

The Flywheel Explosion at the Powerhouse
At 4:45 PM on Wednesday, May 2, 1906, the flywheel at the powerhouse worked loose and went flying out of the wall and ceiling of the building. Fortunately, nobody was injured but the accident was costly. The 20-foot diameter flywheel in the powerhouse on the northwest corner of Main and Sixth in Mansfield was used for the main engine and had several mechanical purposes, including smoothing out power distribution, storing power, and using that stored power in the case of a service interruption. The flywheel in a powerhouse typically was spinning very quickly and something gave way and the flywheel got loose and disconnected. The kinetic energy sent it out of the wall and part of the ceiling. The bigger problems included the stoppage of streetcars and interurbans and the inability to provide electricity for their street lighting contract. Estimates of the damage ranged from $60,000 to $100,000. Meanwhile, temporary repair parts were provided by the Ohio Brass Company so that at least some limited service could be maintained. Service was greatly hampered until the new flywheel was installed in June.

On Thursday May 17, 1906, an interesting situation occurred at the Spring Mill bridge. As the 3:45 car from Mansfield to Shelby was approaching the Pennsylvania Railroad overpass, the motorman noticed a fire had broken out somewhere on top of the bridge. By good fortune there happened to be 4 or 5 empty milk cans on the car, so the motorman and conductor filled them with water in a nearby stream. They ran the car up to the bridge and miraculously got the fire under control.

On July 9, 1906, motorman Frank Sipe got roughed up in Shelby. According to police reports, a Mr. C. J. Barry was waiting at a street in Shelby for a car. A car in the charge of motorman Frank Sipe came by but passed Barry and did not stop to pick him up. This angered Mr. Barry and so he chased down the car when it did stop and gave Sipe quite a beating. He was arrested by Chief Weil of Shelby. He was indicted by a grand jury and held on $200 bond.

Car #44 of the Mansfield and Shelby Electric Railway makes a station stop in Shelby. The first station was located on the northwest corner of Main Street and Mohican Street. Shown here a kind gentleman is helping a lady alight from the car. The station would be located here until November 1912, when it was moved to 16 Mohican Street. The interurban company did not own this building; it was rented. The 1912 depot was built by the interurban company and therefore they had their own waiting room. (Shelby Museum of History)

Another view of the red car #44, this time a beautiful postcard view at the Shelby Big Four Depot. (Shelby Museum of History)

Car #40 poses for an unknown reason on the Pennsylvania Railroad overpass at Spring Mill. The car is southbound heading to Mansfield. (Brent Christy)

852 STREET RAILWAY REVIEW. [Vol. XII, No. 11]

SIGNAL FOR STOPPING INTERURBAN CARS.

A useful device has been patented and placed upon the market by Mr. A. J. Haycox, superintendent of the Citizens Electric Railway, Light & Power Co., of Mansfield, O., the object of which is to enable intending passengers to signal suburban cars at night.

The device, as will be seen from the accompanying illustration, is very simple in design and at the same time is a very necessary adjunct to the suburban railway as it obviates the necessity of passengers lighting matches or burning paper, which are very troublesome expedients for signaling cars on dark nights. The signal box is usually placed above the bracket on a pole near the point where it is desired to stop cars. This signal box is connected by wires to the contact box or switch which is placed about four feet from the

SIGNALLING INTERURBAN CAR AT NIGHT.

ground. The pipe containing the wires is fastened to the pole by staples. By raising the handle the lamps in the signal box are lighted, and but little current is consumed by the device as the lamps remain lighted only while the handle is being held up.

The device, in fact, has the effect of saving power, as without the signal the motorman, not knowing that he is to stop, will leave his controller wide open, and when he sees an intending passenger he is just passing, will throw on the brakes very suddenly to stop the car. In this way he uses current to accelerate his car which would have been unnecessary had he known in advance a stop was to be made. In order to operate a car economically a motorman should know about 1,000 ft. in advance that he has a stop to make and by means of this signal he can handle his car so as not to waste current unnecessarily.

The device consists merely of a group of lamps in the signal box, one end of which is connected permanently to the trolley wire and the other end of the circuit passes to the ground through a switch which is operated by the intending passenger. There is no complication and it is so simple that it is almost impossible for it to get out of order.

The interurban line between Mansfield and Shelby, O., has been equipped with these signals and they have proved entirely satisfactory both to the railway company and its patrons along the line. The device not only saves current and time, but decreases the liability to accidents and avoids the wear and tear on cars and equipment caused by very quick stopping.

STREET RAILWAY STRIKE AT GENEVA, SWITZERLAND.

By courtesy of Mr. H. P. Bradford, general manager of the Compagnie Genevoise des Tramways Electriques, Geneva, Switzerland, we have received an account of the labor troubles with which his company has recently had to contend.

This company was formed a few years ago and purchased the existing tram lines in Geneva and the interurban roads in the vicinity which were then operated by steam. Under the new ownership the old lines have been rebuilt and equipped for electricity and a number of new extensions made to small towns in the territory. The first year of operation the return on the capital was but little more than 1 per cent and for the current year will not exceed 2 per cent. The stockholders of the company were insistent upon the property paying a better revenue and one of the results was the resignation of the manager and the appointment of Mr. Bradford as his successor. Mr. Bradford took charge August 16th and having in mind the necessity of reducing expenses, on August 30th published an order discharging 44 employes to take effect September 12th. On the following day a general strike of the men was declared, the total number quitting service being 489. The sympathy of the public was with the strikers, doubtless to some extent because of the fact that Mr. Bradford was a foreigner and also because Switzerland is the home of many socialists and labor agitators who have been driven from other European countries.

On September 1st it was agreed that the questions in dispute should be referred to a commission of three members appointed by the Council of State and on the following day the strikers returned to work pending a decision. This decision was rendered September 12th and was favorable to the employes who obtained a reinstatement of the 44 men discharged and some modifications of the rules to which they objected.

On September 25th a complaint was made to the Council of State by the men, it being alleged that the company was not living up to its agreement. The Council of State heard both sides of the controversy and decided that complaints of the men were without cause. On the 27th of September a strike was ordered for the 28th, but this was not general. A number of cars were sent out that day and more the succeeding day until October 3d when the regular service was given, and the company announced that after that date none of the old men would be reinstated.

The first few days of the strike resulted in but little disturbance but beginning with October 1st it was necessary to call out several companies of militia to suppress disorder. On October 6th it was sufficiently grave for the Council of State of Geneva to issue a proclamation calling attention to the fact that instigators of the trouble were, for the most part, not natives of Geneva and calling on all good citizens to lend their aid in suppressing the disorder.

ELECTRIC RAILWAYS IN SOUTHERN INDIANA.

"There are railroads talked of, dreamed of, surveyed, prospected, promoted—good, bad and indifferent in this community just now.

"What with the Black Diamond, too dead to skin, the Indianapolis Southern past redemption, the Columbus, Brownstown, Salem, Paoli and French Lick Electric Line just sticking up its head, the Jasper, French Lick and Mitchell with its surveyors in the field and courting two routes, the Walsh road from Indian Springs to West Baden, Paoli and down the pike to the River, the Taggart-Buskirk-Dickerson-Fairbanks line up the pike and a Chicago company awfully anxious to build over the same route it begins to look really dangerous to life and limb, they are so awfully thick.

"But, of course, they won't all get here at once—come gradually perhaps, so that we can become some accustomed to the whiz and roar and clang and bang and be able, with a little time and education, to keep off the numerous tracks and thereby save our scalps."
—Fredericksburg (Ind.) Gazette.

Street Railway Review article published in November 1902 explaining the innovative stop lights on the M&S interurban line. (Street Railway Review Volume XII, No. 11)

Innovation on the Mansfield & Shelby Electric Railway

According to the *Street Railway Review, Volume 12, Number 11* (published in November of 1902), the M&S line developed an innovation for passengers. Stop lights were placed at rural stops along the route that could be activated by waiting passengers at night. The passenger could open a box which contained a switch. The switch worked much like a normal light switch and when turned "on" a light would activate on the pole. This way the motorman would know that there was a waiting passenger. A. J. Haycox, the manager of the Citizen's Electric Railway, Light and Power Company indicated to the *Street Railway Review* that the purpose was simply to "enable intending passengers to signal a suburban car at night." The device was also patented. It didn't last long, however. The power source was from the overhead feeder line and if there was significant moisture in the ground the system could "short out" as this design was rudimentary and could be a safety concern.

The Sandusky, Norwalk, and Mansfield Electric Railway

Much had been written about the potential connection of the M&S line to a connecting line north of Shelby to ultimately reach Sandusky and Lake Erie. Another interurban line, the Sandusky, Norwalk, and Mansfield Electric Railway had been constructed from Norwalk south to Plymouth with a branch over to Chicago Junction from a point called Newman's. The line opened to the public on July 1, 1905. The SN&M had always intended to extend south to Shelby to connect with the M&S line, but resources were scarce. In fact, the M&S had considered extending north to Plymouth themselves over the years (up until 1907) to connect with the SN&M there. At any rate, the SN&M formed a subsidiary company called the Plymouth and Shelby Traction Company in 1905, secured the bonds, and began constructing south to Shelby from Plymouth. Construction was very slow and piecemeal and it seemed like forever until the line reached the corner of Second Street and East Smiley Avenue in Shelby. It was "stuck" there for a while until an agreement could be made with the B&O Railroad in Shelby for a crossing. Even worse, the M&S line already owned the tracks from that point on East Smiley and south on Mohican Street to the depot. A new franchise and ordinance needed to be issued and that took quite some time. On April 4, 1907, SN&M cars were operating out of Shelby from the Second Street/East Smiley intersection north to Plymouth. By May 4, 1907, the crossing over the B&O had been completed and the trackage rights agreement with the M&S was secured. SN&M cars could now operate from the Shelby interurban depot all the way to Plymouth. The first schedule was issued that day and cars did indeed begin normal operations. More importantly, a "wye track" was constructed on Mohican Street just north of Whitney. The wye track extended east into a small lot sold to the SN&M on April 13 by the Sutter Furniture Company. The wye track allowed cars heading northbound to pull in and back out to face southbound (and vice versa). Even though the M&S cars were double-ended, the SN&M cars were not, so they had to turn around at Shelby to head back to Plymouth. For convenience the M&S began using the wye rather than take the time to switch ends and switch the controller. The opening of the SN&M line would prove to be very important, at least for a few years, because now cars, if desired, could be run through from Mansfield to Sandusky by operating over the M&S to Shelby, the SN&M to Norwalk, and the Lake Shore Electric Railway to Sandusky.

Cleveland Southwestern & Columbus Electric Railway

Because the Cleveland Southwestern had gained control of the MRL&P system in Mansfield by default they gained control of the Mansfield & Shelby Electric Railway. In a sense, it was really the Southwestern controlling the interurban line behind the scenes. On July 6, 1907, the Cleveland Southwestern purchased 5,025 shares of common stock of the MRL&P out of the 10,000 available, thus giving the CSW a controlling interest. For the most part, other than officers and operating territories, this wasn't noticed much. However, since the Cleveland Southwestern & Columbus Railway merged with the Ohio Central Traction, the OCT'S ticket office and waiting room was moved out of Ozier's Cigar Store at 7 North Main and into the common depot at 3 North Main Street in Mansfield on May 29, 1907. In addition, S. A. Foltz was made general manager of both the city lines and the Shelby interurban and also the division superintendent of the entire former Ohio Central Traction from Mansfield to Bucyrus.

Cleveland Southwestern car #136 waits at the 3 North Main Street depot location. (Timothy Brian McKee)

Electric Package Agency

Late in December of 1907, it was decided by the MRL&P that the M&S interurban line would no longer operate their own freight service but would join what was called the Electric Package Agency. The EPA could be thought of as sort of a modern-day trucking company. A group of interurban companies grouped together to establish set freight rates. More importantly, it would allow any freight run designated as EPA to continue right along onto another company's tracks so long as they were a participating member of the EPA. As for the M&S, unfortunately the SN&M was not a participating member. The SN&M was a Wells Fargo carrier its entire life and never participated in the EPA. The freight car on the M&S to Shelby and back ceased running December 27, 1907. The EPA took effect on January 1, 1908. The EPA depot was located in Mansfield on the square at 22 South Park Street. Two round trips per day ran to Shelby and back. The freight was transferred at Mansfield to a Cleveland Southwestern interurban freight car and that car typically ran to Cleveland. When the Columbus-Bucyrus interurban line was completed, freight could then go to Columbus, Dayton, or Cincinnati via Bucyrus. The freight car used on the Shelby line is not known but it is very likely it was provided by the MRL&P city line or the Cleveland Southwestern, or both. Freight could be picked up at the Shelby depot and at the EPA depot at 22 South Park Street. If any Wells Fargo freight from the SN&M needed to be forwarded to Mansfield there were sometimes special runs made dedicated for this service.

In the above EPA ticket the CSW represents the M&S because they had a controlling interest. (Timothy Brian McKee)

The Electric Package Agency office in Mansfield was located at 22 South Park Street on the "square". It opened on January 2, 1908, and served as the office in Mansfield until 1921, when it was moved to a new interurban depot at North Diamond and Third. The Mansfield-Shelby Interurban, as well as the Cleveland Southwestern, called on this office for many, many shipments of LCL, or less-than-carload, freight runs. (The Sherman Room, Mansfield Library)

Louis Straub, who had been in the partnership with Vergil Stanninger in the barber business at 3 ½ North Main Street in Mansfield, had disposed of that business and was appointed the Shelby agent for the Electric Package Agency. He was also appointed assistant ticket agent to Mrs.

Hodges for the Mansfield & Shelby Electric Railway. In Mansfield W. F. Spencer who for the past two years had been a clerk in the office of the Mansfield Railway, Light, and Power Company assumed the additional duties of the local agent (both ticket and Electric Package) for the Cleveland Southwestern. Under these agents, the first full trip occurred on January 2, 1908. Furthermore, likely due to the physical and demanding work of Electric Package and Wells Fargo (SN&M), Mrs. Hodges resigned her position as Shelby agent. On January 28, 1908, Luther Straub took over in Shelby as agent for everything. Because he had to handle tickets for both the M&S and SN&M, Wells Fargo for SN&M, Electric Package for the M&S, and Western Union duties, it is said he worked "round the clock" and lived upstairs in the building. As an aside, although the SN&M did not directly handle Electric Package freight, the Cleveland Southwestern's route from Mansfield to Cleveland had still not been completed by this date. Therefore, the only route for the Southwestern was via the SN&M to Norwalk and then over to Cleveland on their Cleveland-Norwalk line. Electric Package Freight cars of the Southwestern would run on the SN&M until February of 1909 when the Mansfield-Cleveland line was completed.

As will be described in *Part II: The Sandusky, Norwalk, and Mansfield Electric Railway Company*, there was a mysterious freight motor on the SN&M that appeared in mid-1908 and lasted until late 1910, making dedicated freight runs from Mansfield through to Sandusky.

Mansfield Railway, Light & Power Company freight motor shown at the powerhouse in Mansfield. This freight motor was used on the M&S interurban line to Shelby for any and all types of freight runs, including the Electric Package Agency. (Street Railway Review Volume XIV, No. 16)

The Cedar Point Limited

The summer of 1908 was a big season for the M&S, SN&M, and Lake Shore Electric (LSE). In the summer season of 1908, the 3 interurban companies teamed up to run what was called The Limited from Mansfield to Sandusky and back for Cedar Point service. The Lake Shore Electric supplied the car. It left Mansfield at 7:30 A.M. and ran through to Sandusky with only 8 stops along the way. The car ran on the Mansfield-Shelby Electric Railway from Mansfield to Shelby, the SN&M from Shelby to Norwalk, and finally the LSE to the boat pier in Sandusky. Later in the evening the car returned. The first run was Saturday May 2, 1908, and the last run was Labor Day, or September 7, 1908. For an unknown reason the service was not instituted in 1909 or 1910. It resumed for the 1911 summer season. During that season the M&S cars were going to do the honors, but it was the LSE car that actually ran and newspapers referred to it as "the big yellow car." Although the service sounded good, it was surprisingly not very well-patronized and the idea was never revisited. For two summers, however, a big Lake Shore Electric coach would be seen or even ridden, twice per day. Other experiments were tried in 1909-1914 with the M&S and the SN&M. Variations of through-cars were tried from Mansfield to Plymouth, Mansfield to Norwalk, and Shelby to Sandusky (with the LSE). None of them proved satisfactory, so by 1914, all of these "through-runs" were scrapped.

Back on June 6, 1908, unrelated to the Cedar Point and through-service, car #40 of the M&S was repainted. The cars up to this point were dark red. Car #40 came out of the shop painted green. Although not recorded, it is possible that the other two cars, #42 and #44, were also painted green at this time.

Over the next few years things were fairly steady and business was good. Freight business was so good that the M&S had to step in and help out the Wells Fargo business in Mansfield from the railroads. There was so much Wells Fargo business that the M&S had to run special Electric Package Agency cars to handle that load. The Wells Fargo freight that the specials on the M&S would take to Shelby were relayed to the SN&M interurban or run out to the Shelby Big Four depot. The first special car of that type was run on March 12, 1909, and could be run anytime thereafter as required.

Trouble could occur on the interurban line. Early automobiles seemed to have trouble watching out for the interurban cars. On August 19, 1909, an automobile carrying six lady passengers backed onto the right-of-way of the M&S interurban at the Bowman Street crossing where the M&S turned and paralleled the south side of the Pennsylvania Railroad. The car was a touring car in charge of chauffeur Clarence Sigler of Mansfield. The M&S car left Mansfield at 3:00 PM and was headed northbound to Shelby. The party had gone north up to Terman Hill to get a good view of the city. When the party was ready to return, the auto backed up between the Pennsylvania Railroad and the M&S line and as the rear of the car came onto the M&S, the northbound car smacked the auto and sent it into a ditch. The 6 ladies were injured but not fatally. The interurban car backed up with the injured as far as the Bowman Street School where other emergency vehicles were waiting. Mr. Sigler was not injured.

An embarrassing mishap occurred on December 6, 1910. The 7:45 AM car out of Mansfield left the Mohican Street depot, pulled into the wye and backed out to run in reverse out to the Shelby Big Four depot, as was the custom. For some reason, when reaching the stub end of the line at the Big Four depot, it hadn't slowed down much and ran off the track and knocked a hole into the south side of the depot. A passenger car and work car had to come up from Mansfield to get the car back on the track and get it going. It didn't return to Mansfield until 10:15 AM.

More Depot News - Shelby

On April 16, 1912, plans were approved by the MRL&P to build a new ticket office and waiting room in Shelby. Up to this point the company rented out a room on the northwest corner of Main and Mohican. This building would be owned entirely by the MRL&P and was to be located at 16 Mohican Street, north of the original ticket office. Like anything else things moved rather slowly. On September 27, 1912, Manager S. A. Foltz gave some updates. The depot would be much better than the last. There would be a sanitary drinking fountain along with both men's and women's restrooms. A cement walk would be constructed in front of the tracks (Mohican Street hadn't been paved yet), and the depot would be locked at night after the agent left to get rid of loitering bums. The depot finally opened sometime in November of 1912. Louis Straub remained ticket agent for the time being. However, on January 2, 1914 he was promoted to one of 3 agents at Mansfield. His replacement was a gentleman by the name of Albert Gray. Albert Gray did a fantastic job and served faithfully until the Shelby interurban depot ceased to be a ticket and freight office in 1926.

Ownership and Organizational Changes

As far as revenue and passenger ridership were concerned, things continued to go very well for the interurban line. In a complicated court proceeding, the MRL&P, on November 25, 1912, technically went into receivership. Judge Mansfield in Richland County Common Pleas Court ordered the MRL&P dissolved and a receiver to be appointed at a later date. This was not a typical receivership where a company is in money trouble. The common stock holders brought suit against the MRL&P because the Cleveland Southwestern had a controlling interest because it owned 5,025 of the common shares. The claim was made that the earnings the Southwestern was making from its owned shares of the MRL&P were being used illegally to improve the Southwestern's own system. Judge Mansfield agreed. At any rate none of this would end up affecting the operation of the interurban line.

On March 24-25, 1913, rains would not relent and a great flood ensued. This of course became the famous flood of 1913. The only item to mention is the fact that the interurban and streetcar

Like many communities in Ohio, Shelby was a victim of the 1913 flood. This view looks south on Mohican Street from Whitney Avenue. The interurban tracks aren't visible but the overhead wiring is. The pole with the mast arm on the right leaned to the left during the flood, lowering the height of the wire. Fix the pole? Nah. Just bend up the mast arm. A close inspection behind the pole reveals the Wells Fargo Express symbol which the Sandusky, Norwalk, and Mansfield Electric Railway used. The 1912 depot is the big white block building on the right. (Shelby Museum of History)

routes were shut down for several days while waters receded and damaged track and bridges were repaired. There was an improvement made to the interurban on May 17, 1913. Due to the powerhouse continuing to have trouble often enough to disrupt service on the M&S, the Cleveland Southwestern handled the problem. The CSW had a high tension power line strung from Elyria that ran along its route from Polk to Galion. The high tension line bypassed Mansfield since the city streetcar system had its own power. The high tension line ran along Longview Avenue along the north side of Mansfield and rejoined the CSW at Longview and Springmill. The high tension line crossed the M&S right-of-way at Bowman and Longview. Traveling north on the M&S out of Mansfield the track was in the center of Bowman until Longview, where it then went off the street and paralleled the east side of Bowman. At this point Siding #1 was located. The Cleveland Southwestern placed a portable substation on Siding #1 and fed AC current to the substation from the high tension line where it was then converted to 600 DC to be fed into the overhead trolley wire. This would now solve the long-standing "power problem" that the M&S had been experiencing to Shelby. If the powerhouse had trouble, the substation could be turned on manually and the interurban could continue to be powered. Later this substation became so reliable it became the permanent single source of electricity for the M&S until the big MELCO plant was completed and turned on in late 1917.

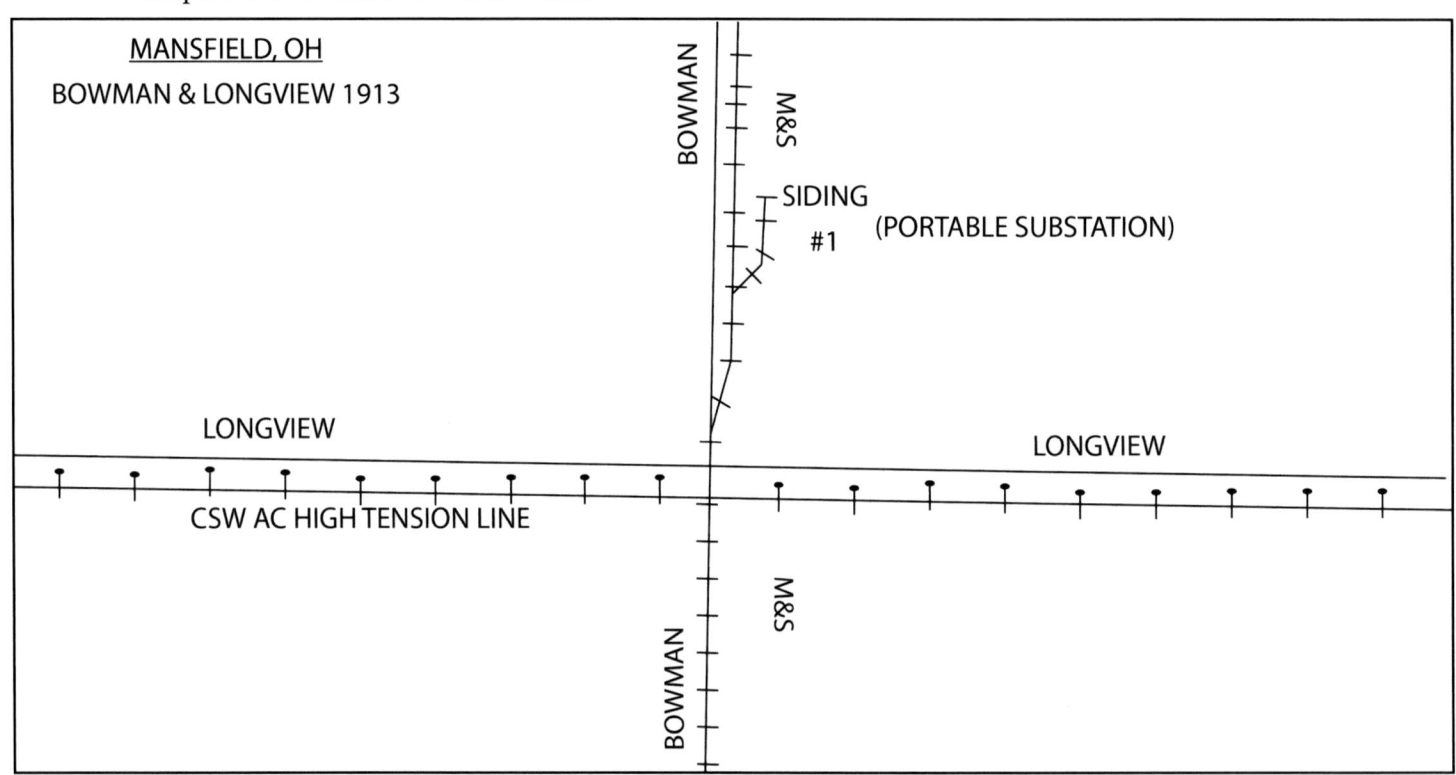

Map detailing the Cleveland Southwestern's high tension AC electric line on the south side of Longview Avenue. The M&S line ran up Bowman and left the street after going under the wires, where Siding #1 was and the portable substation was placed in 1913.

There were two notable improvements for 1914. The first was the purchase by the streetcar company of a line car dedicated specifically for the interurban line. The line car was put into use on August 20, 1914, and was purportedly the best line car in use in the entire area. The second was the new big interurban depot in Mansfield at 48 North Diamond Street. This fine 3-story brick building was located on the northeast corner of North Diamond and East Third Street. It was used only by the interurbans and was not used for city streetcars. A wye track was built east on East Third to Franklin so the big interurban cars could turn around. It was completed on December 28, 1914, and opened the next day for use. This became the famous interurban depot in

The Mansfield interurban depot was designed in 1914. It was built during the year and opened for business on December 29, 1914, on the northeast corner of North Diamond Street and East Third Street. A wye was constructed with a track extending east on Third to Franklin so that the interurban cars could turn around and reverse direction. The depot was used exclusively by interurbans while the streetcars remained at 3 North Main Street. (Timothy Brian McKee)

Postcard view of a Mansfield-Shelby car on the "wye" at the interurban depot in Mansfield. (Timothy Brian McKee)

A Mansfield-Shelby car on North Diamond Street at the interurban depot. (Timothy Brian McKee)

Beautiful interior postcard rendition of the interurban depot in Mansfield. (Timothy Brian McKee)

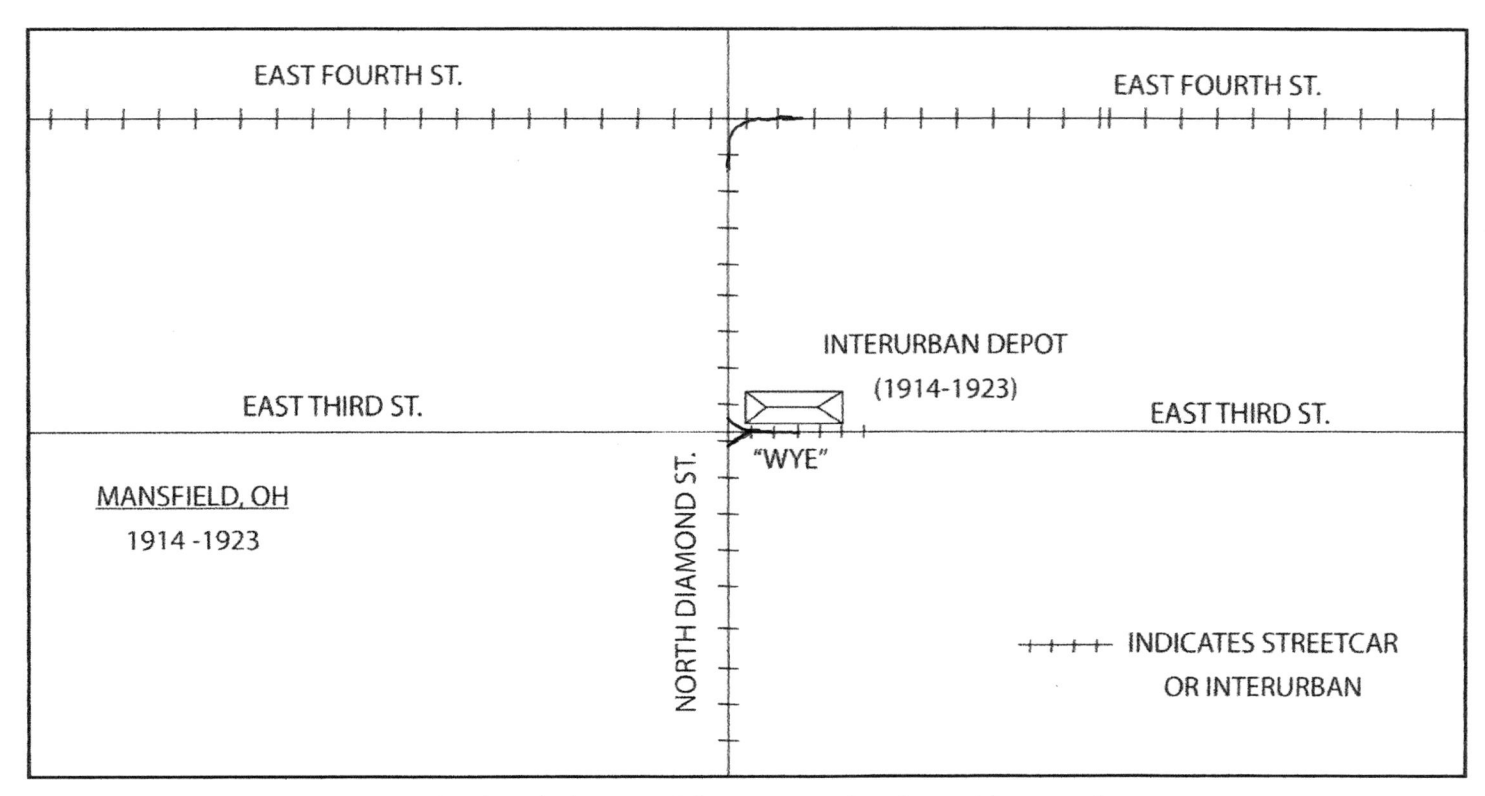

Map detailing the location of the new interurban depot with wye track.

Mansfield-Shelby car #44 on South Park Street in Mansfield in 1914. (Timothy Brian McKee)

Mansfield that citizens came to know and love and will forever be remembered as the "Interurban Depot." It lasted as an interurban depot until September 30, 1923.

The most interesting news in 1915 was the rebuilding of car #44. This car was sent to the Cleveland Southwestern shops in Elyria and was lengthened by 8 feet. It was said to be "modernized" and painted a wine color. Frank Sipe and Albert Keckler did the honors in bringing the car back to Mansfield. All 3 of the M&S cars were lengthened eventually. By 1920, during Richland Public Service days, they had reached their final specifications: #40 went in shortly after #44, and as will be mentioned later, #42 went in during the autumn of 1920.

Another Flywheel Explosion – This Time Fatal

As can be recalled, the powerhouse's main engine had its flywheel crash through the wall and ceiling of the powerhouse in 1906. In that case, nobody was injured. On Friday night, September 22, 1916, an engine's flywheel flew off again; the engine was located in the extreme southwest corner of the building. C. Edward Moore attempted to start this 250-HP engine. The governors on the flywheel would not work for an unknown reason, and before he could turn off the power, the wheel spun out of control. The explosion could be heard blocks away as the flywheel broke into sections with some sections crashing out of the building, through the walls and ceilings.

One piece wrecked the building of Frank Schwein across the street. Tragically, C. Edward Moore of Shelby, the operator, perished in this terrible explosion. L. R. Brubaker, who was also working in the powerhouse, was on the north end and was not affected. Aside from the awful death of Moore, this explosion was far more costly and disruptive of service to the streetcars, the interurban line, and the street lighting than the mishap in 1906.

It must be mentioned briefly that in May of 1917, the Pennsylvania Railroad at Spring Mill wished to add a third track to its mainline arrangement. Therefore the interurban bridge over the PRR would need to be expanded and rebuilt. From May 10 to June 8, 1917, the bridge was quickly rebuilt and made longer. It opened to interurban traffic on June 8. While the bridge was being built passengers were at an inconvenience as they had to walk across the PRR tracks to board a car on the other side of the tracks. Fortunately this arrangement didn't last long.

Unfortunately, more legal wrangling ensued in the years 1915-1918. Some of the most complicated legal and court transactions took place during this period, but only a summarization will be presented. Back on January 13, 1913, president S. N. Ford had been appointed receiver of the MRL&P. Later in 1915, the MRL&P was ordered by the courts to be sold. To do so, an auction was held on September 15, 1915, at the courthouse in Mansfield. Six weeks prior in late July of 1915 a company called the Mansfield Public Utilities & Service was incorporated. The company representative showed up to the auction and purchased the MRL&P for $10,000. Technically the streetcar system and interurban was the MPU&S Company and no longer the MRL&P. However, the company never actually referred to itself as such and continued to operate under the MRL&P name. It took a very long time for all of the property to be transferred to the MPU&S. The last of it was transferred on May 16, 1917. At this time S. A Foltz resigned his position as general manager due to new management coming in and taking control. P. Barnhart of Illinois took his place. S. N. Ford remained president with Frederick Hertenstein of Cincinnati, vice president, and P. Barnhart also as secretary and treasurer. Reid Carpenter of Mansfield and Henry Hoppe of Cincinnati would comprise the board of directors.

The biggest change was when Henry Doherty & Company of New York, who also owned the Cities Service Company, came in and purchased all of the MPU&S property. The Cities Service Company was simply a big holding company which owned and controlled public utility, oil, and gas properties. Henry L. Doherty & Company were the operators of the holding company. The new streetcar,

This spectacular view was taken from the top of a B&O boxcar in Shelby on Smiley Avenue. The track to the right is the M&S interurban line peeling off Smiley and heading north to the Big Four depot. The SN&M is running left to right on Smiley and the famous Spring Hinge building is in the background. (Shelby Museum of History)

Mansfield & Shelby Electric Railway car #44 northbound along the Black Fork in Shelby. (Shelby Museum of History)

interurban, and power companies would be under the ownership of the Mansfield Electric, Light & Power Company. The first item was to build a large power generating plant in the area. This was built southeast of Lucas at the confluence of the Clear Fork and the Black Fork, famously known as the MELCO Plant for the abbreviation of the full name of the company. The Public Utilities Commission of Ohio approved this big merger on February 23, 1918. Henry Doherty & Company decided to name the company The Richland Public Service Company. New franchises and ordinances were put into place and all were effective by September 1918. It should be obvious that the Cleveland Southwestern at this time no longer had any controlling interest in the property and that topic never resurfaced. The company was serious about service and equipment improvements. All cars were painted with the title "Richland Public Service."

Back on December 8, 1917, the big MELCO plant southeast of Lucas was put into operation and began supplying power to the city streetcar system as well as the M&S interurban. City lighting and consumer power was also sold. The substation on Bowman Street on Siding #1 was not needed any longer by the M&S. The main substation for the AC electricity coming from MELCO was at the corner of East Fifth and North Adams Street (northeast corner) in Mansfield. Later, a bigger substation was built at Olivesburg Road and Longview Avenue. This substation is still there and used today albeit in modern form.

Other than the cars being "stenciled" in Richland Public Service lettering service on the interurban line remained the same. However, it was in 1918 that trouble from the competing automobile began to be felt. Profits slowly declined beginning around this time and did so all the way until 1934. This was true, however, for all interurbans across Ohio, as well as many streetcar systems.

There are no details about this wreck but on November 29, 1918, a car on the M&S line derailed at the PRR overpass at Spring Mill and 22 passengers were injured. It was not uncommon for big heavy coaches to derail on sharp curves built to "streetcar standards."

The year 1919 was very interesting for the M&S. In addition to the Electric Package Agency freight service, a new "special freight service" was inaugurated in the spring of 1919. This freight service hauled any freight and connected to the Cleveland Southwestern in Mansfield. The actual service began in May of 1919.

Simultaneously, car #44 was overhauled and rebuilt again, this time for an unknown reason. Unfortunately there are no records of exactly what was done.

Old Powerhouse Burns

On the night of December 13, 1919, the old powerhouse at the corner of Main and Sixth caught fire and burned completely to the ground. No cause was assigned but it destroyed $100,000 worth of the Richland Public Service's equipment, not to mention the building cost. The old powerhouse as mentioned was being phased out by MELCO, so there were no known service interruptions. It was sad to see the landmark destroyed, however.

In to 1920

On May 7, 1920, this new freight business was really taking off and seemed to please local businesses very much. Two shipments were run out of Shelby to Mansfield. The Shelby Supply and Manufacturing Company sent an entire car load of chewing gum to Mansfield to be relayed to the Erie and Pennsylvania Railroads. Later that day The Ohio Seamless Tube Company or "Tuby" sent out 40,000 lbs. of tubes to be delivered to the White Motor Company of Cleveland. This big load was transferred to the Cleveland Southwestern at Mansfield. The local agent at Shelby, Albert Gray, was kept very busy with this service. Three days later, on May 10, 1920, the Tuby again shipped out 40,000 lbs. of tubes to Cleveland. On May 21, 1920, 50,000 lbs. were shipped to Cleveland. All of these big shipments went to the White Motor Company which obviously had a big special order during those weeks. A May 28, 1920, *Shelby Daily Globe* article indicated that several car loads of freight were being shipped into and out of Shelby on a daily basis.

On November 29, 1920, car #42 was released from the shops; it had been overhauled and rebuilt much like #44 in May of 1919. It was said that the car was rebuilt entirely so that it would be difficult to recognize. The car would accommodate 48 passengers very comfortably and a Smith heater had been installed. During this improvement #42 was lengthened.

Trouble at Shelby

The tragic event in 1921 occurred specifically on March 25, 1921. The Sandusky, Norwalk, and Mansfield Electric Railway was officially abandoned in its entirety from Norwalk south to Shelby, along with its extension from Newman's over to Willard (Chicago Junction became Willard in 1917). By this time, however, it didn't really affect the M&S because service on the SN&M had become so deplorable and sparse not many passengers were surprised. The rail in Shelby wasn't removed but the crossing over the New York Central Big Four was. The SN&M had been purchasing their power from the Cleveland Southwestern and were so far behind on bills that the CSW was shutting off the power on March 25 regardless. The story of the SN&M doesn't end there and will be revisited later. However, this ultimately ended the M&S's connection to the lake.

In 1918, the operations were taken over by the Richland Public Service Company. The cars were repainted reflecting the ownership. Shown here is #40 creeping along grass-carpeted right-of-way up to the Shelby Big Four depot along the Baltimore and Ohio Railroad. The #40 by this time had been lengthened from its original size. (Shelby Museum of History)

Also in 1921, the Electric Package Agency moved from 22 South Park Street to the interurban depot at 48 North Diamond Street in Mansfield. Apparently Mansfield citizens were complaining of traffic tie ups during loading and unloading at Central Park. The EPA was officially moved on June 2, 1921.

A big change occurred on or about March 1, 1922. Another larger public utilities, gas, fuel, and electricity company had been formed through the merger of several other companies and was named the Ohio Public Service Company. Henry L. Doherty & Company controlled this as well. It was their intention to merge all of their holdings into this Ohio Public Service Company, and that's what happened on March 1. It wasn't all done at once, however. The process was done piecemeal from March 1 to December 28. At that point the official full ordinance for the streetcar system and the interurban was granted. The cars however had begun to be repainted with Ohio Public Service letters instead of Richland Public Service. The operations on the M&S didn't change much and remained much the same. At least for a while.

The year 1922 also saw another bizarre event in Shelby. A group of capitalists decided to purchase the old SN&M property and instead of running electric interurban cars they decided to operate gasoline-powered interurban cars. They purchased two of them from the American Car Company in Elyria and numbered them 1 and 2. The company was incorporated as the Norwalk and Shelby Railroad Company. The right-of-way was put back in order but no overhead wire was necessary. There was big trouble in trying to reinstall the Big Four diamond north of Shelby, so they had to compromise. A temporary wye track was built along State Street north of Shelby just north of the Big Four crossing. Cars would come down from Norwalk and a bus or taxi would wait on State Street for the gas car and transfer passengers into the Shelby depot that way. On January 20, 1923, the Big Four crossing was installed and then cars could operate to the Shelby depot on Mohican Street. The temporary wye was removed at State Street and the cars used the normal Mohican Street wye. A gasoline pump was installed at the Shelby interurban depot by the Standard Oil Company so that the cars could refuel.

From 1922 to 1924, there were three wrecks involving M&S cars on Mohican Street in Shelby. On August 14, 1922, car #44 derailed at the wye switch at 8:42 AM. The car wasn't able to leave Shelby until 9:20 AM but operations went on as normal thereafter. On June 20, 1923, car #42 also jumped the track at the wye switch at 4:00 AM. There was a gasoline Norwalk car coming down from Plymouth that had to be held on East Smiley because the main track was blocked. On July 30, 1924, the 6:40 AM car for Mansfield derailed at the wye and went as a runaway car down by the interurban depot. There was a Cline Taxi sitting on Mohican that was badly damaged by the derailed car. Other trouble occurred July 17, 1924, when the north fill approach of the overpass at Spring Mill caught on fire. Apparently it was kept well under control and extinguished.

The interurban depot in Mansfield had been a very popular place with interurban patrons. However, by 1923 ridership had fallen so much that a building the size of the depot was no longer necessary. Sadly on October 1, 1923, the interurban depot at 48 North Diamond was abandoned by the Ohio Public Service. The new depot would be a rented store-front affair at 25 East Fourth Street which was located between North Main and North Diamond, on the north side of the street. Even worse the track east on South Park Street and north on North Diamond to East Fourth was no longer necessary. This stretch of track was removed in 1923 and 1924. To turn interurban cars a new wye was built down Scott Street out at the East Fourth Street car barns and was known simply as the Scott Street wye. For interurban cars to turn eastbound onto East Fourth from North Main Street and vice versa, a new "connection" track had to be built at the Main and Fourth intersection so cars could switch directly southbound to eastbound (and vice versa). The M&S cars always turned east

A Cleveland Southwestern car climbs the Main Street hill southbound toward the photographer about 1908. In the distance a Mansfield city streetcar is following. Main Street was "double-tracked" from Park Avenue West north to a point just beyond Fourth Street approximately in 1905. (Sherman Room, Mansfield Library)

onto Fourth to stop at the depot. They then ran east to the Scott Street wye to turn around and head back to Shelby.

A very big problem with buses poaching interurban traffic in Shelby began in 1923. Drivers of the Red Star Bus Lines were stopping near the corner of Main and Mohican just ahead of the interurban car arrivals to lure passengers to ride the bus instead of the interurban. This problem was not unique to Shelby in that this was happening all over the United States. On July 30, 1923 Shelby City Council passed on ordinance making this illegal and limited the streets the buses could use and also when passengers could be boarded.

A Note About Freight in Mansfield

The freight situation at this point in Mansfield should be mentioned briefly. In late 1916, the Cleveland Southwestern had built their own freight depot, separate from the Electric Package Agency, at the East Fourth Street car barns (one building due west of the car barns). This was used only for what was called "fast freight" service put on by the CSW. The M&S did not participate in this. The CSW, however, still used 22 South Park Street for EPA freight and likewise used the Diamond Street location for their EPA freight when the EPA office moved. When ohe interurban depot on North Diamond Street was closed, the freight depot at the car barns was used by both interurbans and for EPA – EPA for both the CSW and M&S and "fast freight" for the CSW. The "special freights" that the M&S ran were always relayed to the CSW at the freight house at the car barns. This complicated arrangement was difficult to understand. The passenger depots were always at separate locations.

Time Goes On

Back in Shelby on August 17, 1924, the poor Norwalk and Shelby Railroad gave up the ghost and quit for good. Tracks were removed from the switch at Mohican Street Extension with the M&S line all the way to Norwalk in August 1924.

As interurban ridership decreased so did required equipment to operate an interurban. A big blow to the M&S came in August of 1924. It was announced that beginning on November 1, 1924, the 3 plush Kuhlman coaches, #40, #42, and #44 would be scrapped or sold and all 3 of them would be replaced by a single one-man operated car. Ironically this car was also from the G. C. Kuhlman Car Company and was numbered 41. The car would seat 44 people: 28 in the front and 16 in the rear smoking compartment. The car was single-ended meaning it operated from only one end and passengers entered the front door next to the motorman like a bus. There was to be only one crew member who acted as both motorman and conductor. This lone car would operate the M&S until the end in 1934.

Car #42 lasted into Ohio Public Service days, but not for long. It was quickly scrapped in 1924 in favor of the one-man car. #42 is shown here at the Scott Street wye on East Fourth Street in Mansfield in 1922. (Bill Volkmer Collection)

On April 1, 1924, Albert "Bert" Keckler, who was conductor on the first car over to Shelby from Mansfield back in 1901, retired from service. It is calculated that he would have traveled around the world 48 times based upon how many runs he made over the approximately 23 years.

Ridership continued to plummet on the M&S and the company decided that the depot at 16 Mohican Street in Shelby was no longer needed. It would be cheaper to rent a store front much like they had been doing in Mansfield. In late 1925, it was announced that the interurban depot in Shelby on Mohican Street would be closed. R. L. Harbaugh, secretary of the Ohio Public Service and Walter Goodenough, general superintendent, made final arrangements on November 18, 1925, to move the waiting room one door to the south to 14 Mohican Street in the Phillip Julian Restaurant at "The Big Store." No tickets would be sold there but passengers could wait inside. Tickets had to be purchased from the motorman/conductor on the one-man car. The depot at 16 Mohican closed and the waiting room at 14 opened on January 1, 1926. S. A. Foltz still owned the building at 16 and it would be put up for rent thereafter. Albert Gray, the ticket agent at Shelby also had no role there anymore as the cars on the M&S line became PAYE (Pay-As-You-Enter) cars and no ticket agent was needed. He was much appreciated by the Ohio Public Service Company so they promoted him into the general offices of the OPS in Mansfield. Sadly, when the ticket office and EPA office closed in Shelby, so did all freight on the M&S line. The last package freight that was handled was December 31, 1925, but likely not much for that day.

The only event in 1927 was the continual decline in passenger revenue on the M&S. The Ohio Public Service had already closed the Reformatory Line in Mansfield and had replaced the street cars out to the Reformatory with buses. Roads were improving and people were buying more and more automobiles.

G. C. Kuhlman Car Company builder's photo of the one-man car, #41, manufactured for the Mansfield-Shelby interurban. The Richland Public service had already gone to all one-man cars on the city streetcar system in Mansfield as early as 1919. (Bill Volkmer Collection)

In 1928, it was clear that the Electric Package Agency as it was known would be no more. Several participating interurban lines were either abandoned entirely or they were giving up on freight service. Mansfield decided to join what was called the the Universal Carloading and Distributing Company. This was a direct replacement for all of the freight service handled by the interurban and was designed to provide cheap rates for LCL or "less-than-carload" shipments. The CSW partnered with the city of Mansfield and the traffic managers division of the Manufacturers Club, the Mansfield Chamber of Commerce, and the Central Ohio Manufacturers Association. The first shipment to Cleveland was made on the CSW from Mansfield on February 3, 1928. Later that year, in November, the EPA did dissolve and was replaced by the Electric Railways Freight Company. However, the CSW did not participate and remained in the Universal Company.

Another minor note in Mansfield: For an unknown reason the interurban depot moved again. This time the waiting room was moved east to 53 East Fourth Street effective January 1, 1928. The location was on the north side of East Fourth between North Diamond Street and Franklin on the first floor of the Kern Building. That would be the last location of the interurban depot in Mansfield before they were both abandoned.

G. C. Kuhlman "side-view" builder's photo of the one-man car. (Shelby Museum of History)

The Richland Public Service and Ohio Public Service employed one-man cars in Mansfield after 1919. Here is a Birney car in O.P.S. days at the "steel mill stop" which was located on Bowman at Pomerene. This service was designed to help workers come to and from work and schedules were synched up with shift changes as best as possible. (Columbus Public Library)

The End

In 1929, after the Great Depression hit, the interurban world was shaken. In 1930, the Cleveland Southwestern freight interchange to Columbus was wiped out by the abandonment of the Columbus, Marion, and Bucyrus Electric Railway. Freight had been being shipped rather successfully from Cleveland and Mansfield to Columbus, Dayton, and Cincinnati via that connection in Bucyrus. With that gone the CSW really had nothing else to look forward to as profits from passengers were literally null by that point. On January 31, 1931, the Cleveland Southwestern folded and abandoned their system. The M&S now could only connect to the streetcar system in Mansfield, which was also suffering. This didn't help matters on the M&S. According to officials the last full year where a profit was made every month on the M&S was way back in 1918.

On January 9, 1934, the Ohio Public Service petitioned the Public Utilities Commission of Ohio to abandon the M&S interurban in its entirety from Mansfield to Shelby Junction. A hearing was set and on February 16, 1934, the PUCO granted the OPS permission to abandon the line. The last car left Shelby on February 28, 1934, at 10:35 PM in the one-man Kuhlman car, #41, in the charge of motorman C. W. Curtiss. For Mansfield and Shelby that meant the end of the interurban era.

M&S interurban track along the Black Fork in O.P.S. days (1928). This view looks west out of the Shelby High School building prior to W. W. Skiles football field being completed. (Shelby Museum of History)

Next year, 1929, the approximate same view was taken after W. W. Skiles field had been built. First football game was in October of 1929. (Shelby Museum of History)

Fantastic postcard view of the Electric Lamp Works and the interurban track as it turns onto Mack Avenue. (Shelby Museum of History)

Brilliant photo of Shelby High School sometime after 1926. The interurban and overhead wire are seen on the left. (Shelby Museum of History)

One of the last runs to Shelby in 1934 on the one-man lightweight Kuhlman car #41. The car is westbound on West Sixth Street in Mansfield between North Main and Mulberry. Note the streetcar in the background on Main. (VanTilberg Collection)

Last Car on Shelby-Mansfield Line Runs Wednesday Night, February 28:

Street car service on the Shelby-Mansfield line will be discontinued Wednesday night, February 28 at 12 o'clock. The Ohio Public Service Company was granted permission to abandon this line as the company has been operating at a loss for many years.

The Buckeye Stages Inc., has been granted a license by the Utilities Commission to operate a bus line between Shelby and Mansfield. This company will start their service on March 1, so that there will be no interruption of service between the two cities. The bus company will have their waiting station at the H. L. Crowell drug store at the corner of West Main and Gamble street. R. W. Miller, representing the Buckeye Stages Inc., was in Shelby today and completed all arrangements for starting the bus line.

Busses will leave Shelby daily at 7, 8, 9:09, 10, 12, 1:09, 2, 4, 4:30, 5.09, 5:30, 7, 9 and 10:30. On Saturday evening there will be a late bus out of Shelby for Mansfield at 12 o'clock.

Busses will leave Mansfield at 6, 7, 9, 9:30, 11, 1, 1:30, 3, 4, 5, 5:30, 6, 8 and 9:30 o'clock. On Saturday night there will be a late bus leaving Mansfield for Shelby at 11:30 o'clock.

Shelby Daily Globe, February 26, 1934
On March 1, 1934, the Buckeye Stages, an incorporated bus company, took over the interurban business. The bus station in Shelby was at the H. L. Crowell drug store at Gamble and Main.
The M&S rails were scrapped for the metal but many Shelby citizens remembered the concrete strips on Mack and Tucker Avenues that remained for years, reminding us of a lost mode of transportation.

The Mansfield-Shelby interurban car #41, the Kuhlman one-man lightweight, is seen pulling south along Scott Street to turn on the wye in 1928. East Fourth can be seen in the background. (Bill Volkmer Collection)

Forlorn car #44 sitting along the car barns in Mansfield at East Fourth and Scott. As can be clearly seen, #44 had been lengthened by 8 feet in 1915 (from its original M&S dimensions). Car #44 wouldn't last much longer from this 1928 date. (Bill Volkmer Collection)

Almost as if waving goodbye, this gentleman is on #41 at the Shelby Big Four depot in the waning days of the interurban line in approximately 1932. The right-of-way is very typical of many interurbans in Ohio at this time: grass-carpeted and weed-grown. The sign on the car is for Barbara Stanwyck with lead man George Brent at the Ohio Theater in Mansfield. (Shelby Museum of History)

Hazel's Diner - Corner of Main & Mohican Streets

Not all interurban and streetcars were scrapped. Many were repurposed. Hazel's Diner existed in Shelby on the northwest corner of Main and Mohican, fittingly where the original depot had sat. It was owned and operated by Woodrow and Hazel Shaw. Opening day for Hazel's was October 29, 1946. On March 14, 1956, it burned and the insurance coverage provided for a new building. The old structure was sold and repaired and on April 8, 1956, it was moved to Elm Street and used as a residence. Ironically, on November 14, 1956, the structure again caught fire but this time burned to the ground. The diner is believed to have been an interurban car, #51 of the Columbus, Delaware, and Marion Electric Railway, an interurban line that operated from Columbus to Marion and Bucyrus. (Shelby Museum of History)

This aerial photo in Shelby is looking northeast on the southeast side of town. At the bottom is the intersection of Mack and Tucker Avenue. A close inspection reveals the two concrete "strips" traveling south on Mack, east on Tucker, then south between Jenner and the B&O RR, a reminder of the Mansfield-Shelby interurban line. (Shelby Museum of History)

KEY MAPS ALONG THE M&S ROUTE

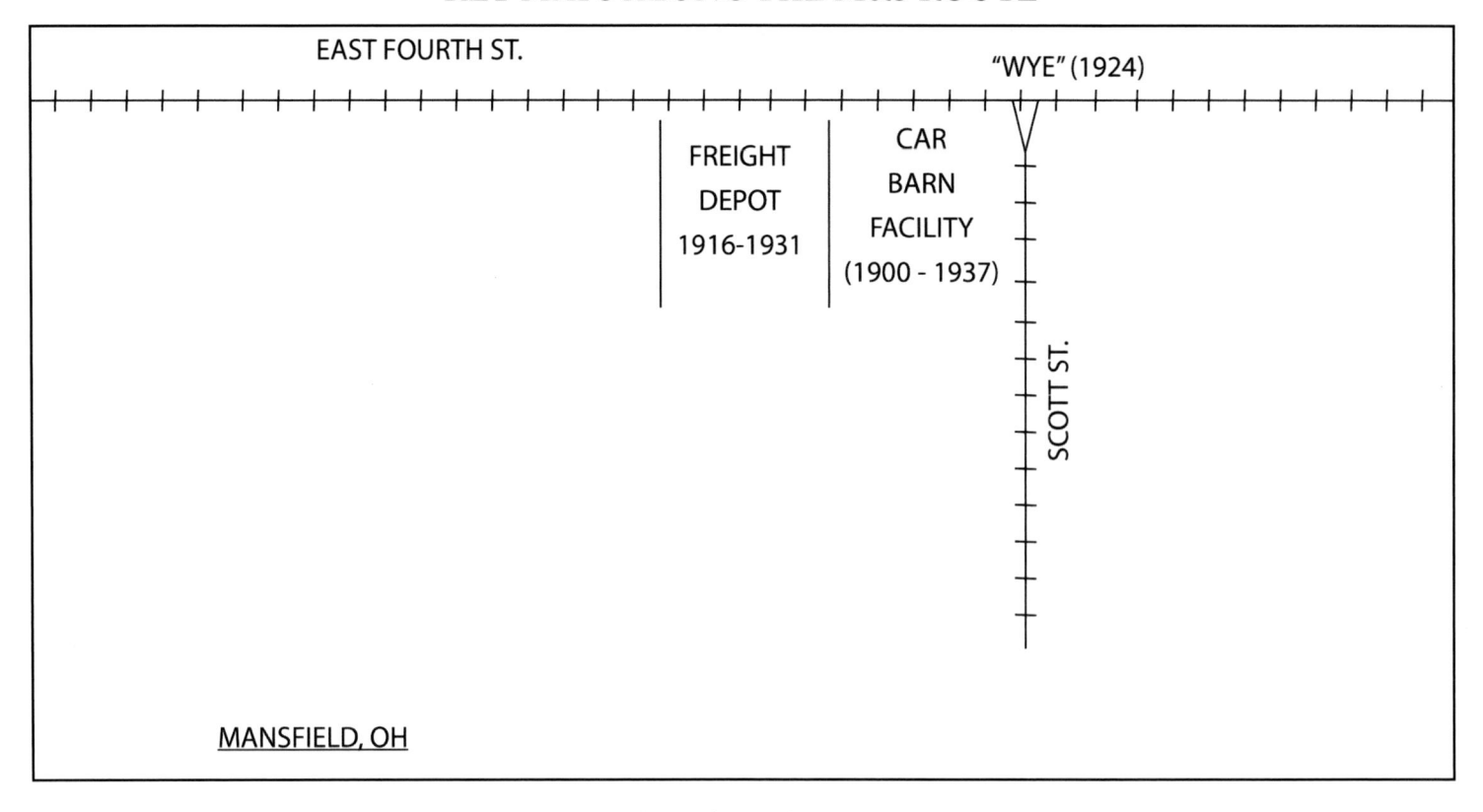

```
EAST FOURTH ST.                    "WYE" (1924)

                FREIGHT      CAR
                DEPOT        BARN
                1916-1931    FACILITY
                             (1900 - 1937)
                                              SCOTT ST.



MANSFIELD, OH
```

East Fourth Street car barns and 1916 freight depot at East Fourth and Scott Streets.

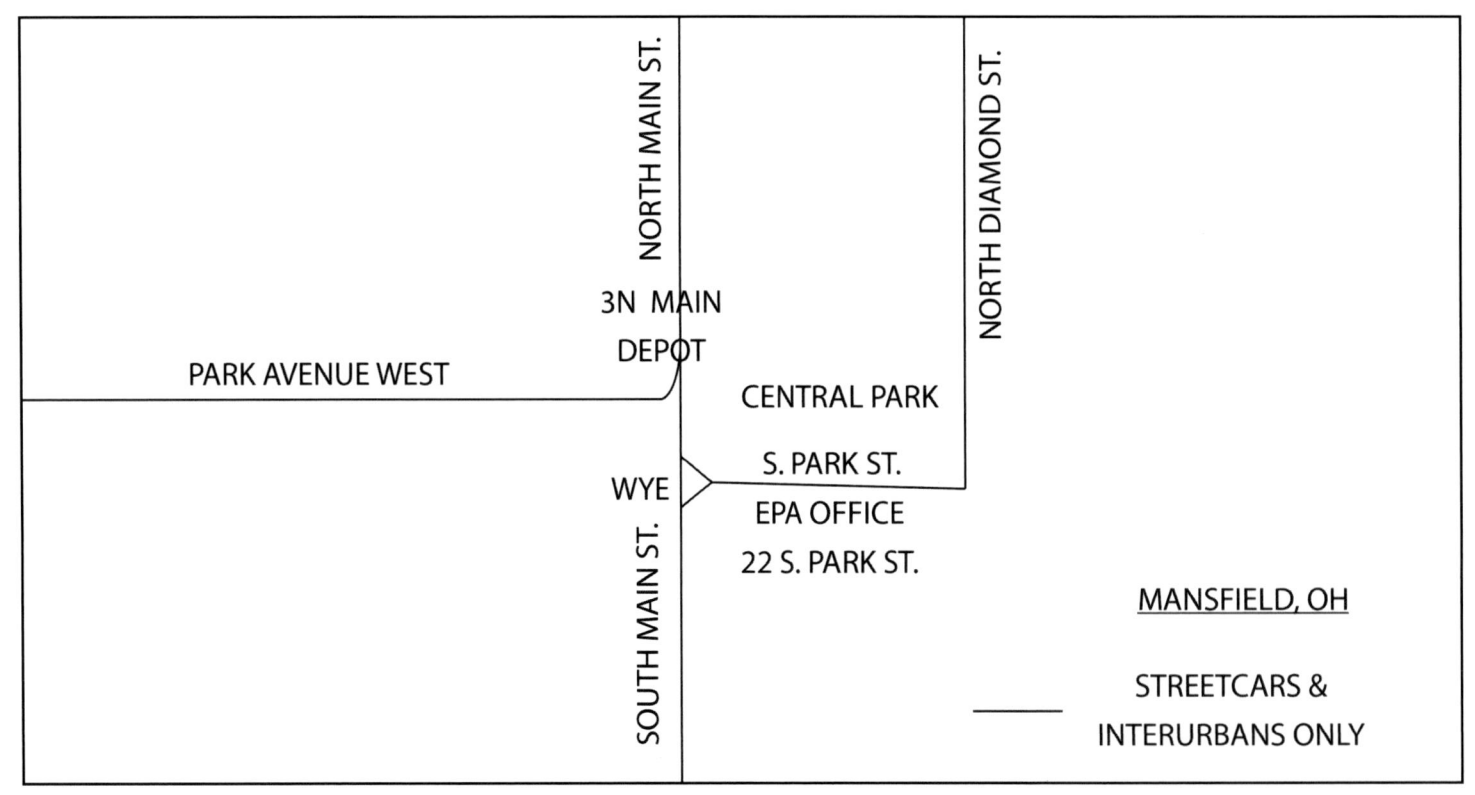

```
                    NORTH MAIN ST.      NORTH DIAMOND ST.


                        3N MAIN
PARK AVENUE WEST        DEPOT
                                    CENTRAL PARK
                                    S. PARK ST.
                        WYE >       EPA OFFICE
                                    22 S. PARK ST.
                    SOUTH MAIN ST.                      MANSFIELD, OH

                                                        STREETCARS &
                                                        INTERURBANS ONLY
```

All-Time downtown Mansfield Map. Streetcar/interurban routes shown only. This layout was during the height of streetcar/interurban days. The track was constructed down South Park Street and up North Diamond in 1908 and removed in early 1924. The 1905 interurban depot and the streetcar depot was at 3 North Main and until 1921 the Electric Package Agency was at 22 South Park Street. The wye on South Park Street was built in November of 1902.

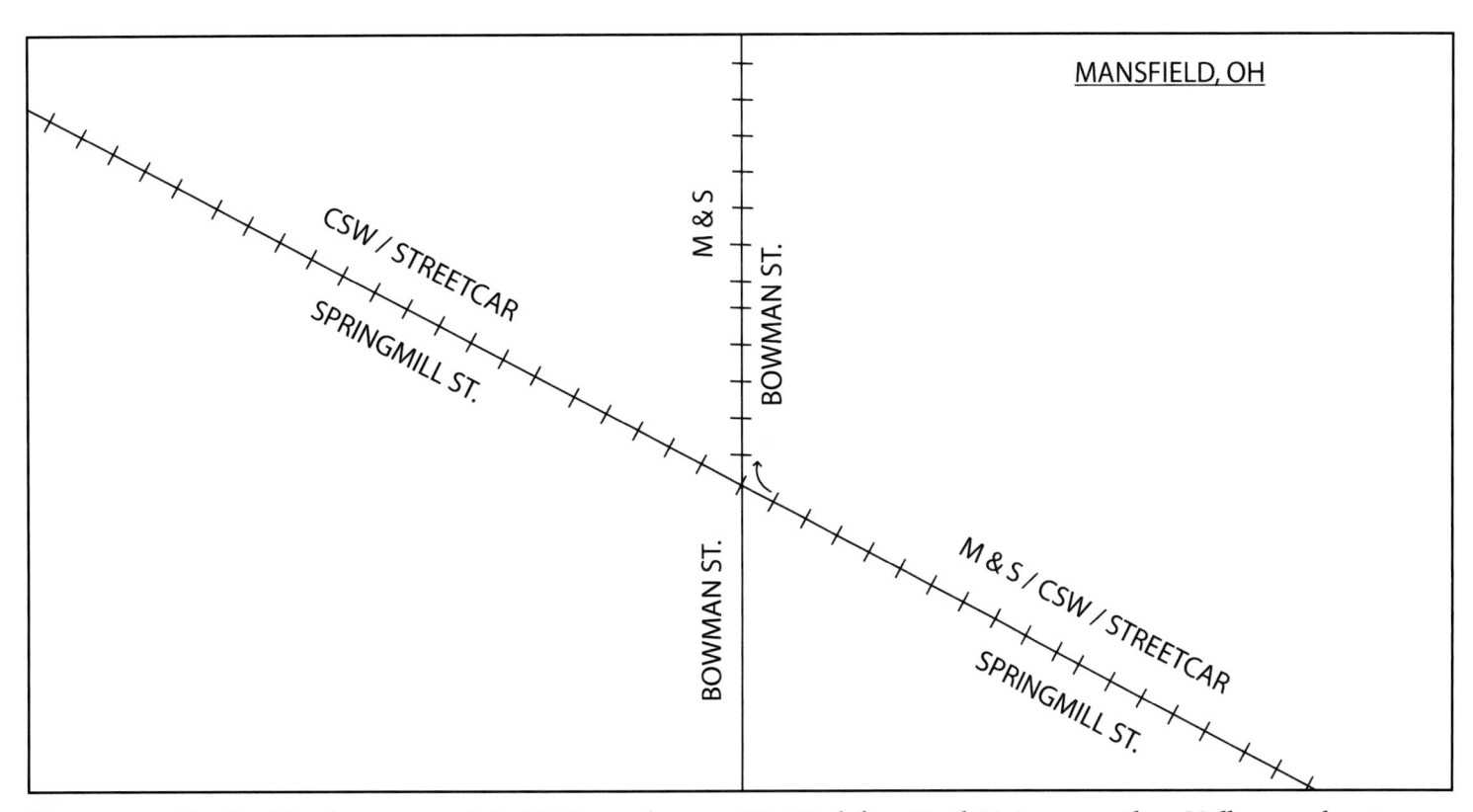

The streetcar, Cleveland Southwestern, and the M&S turned west on West Sixth from North Main, ran north on Mulberry and west on Springmill. At Bowman Street the M&S turned north while the streetcar system continued out to Burns at the original fairgrounds and the Cleveland Southwestern to Bucyrus.

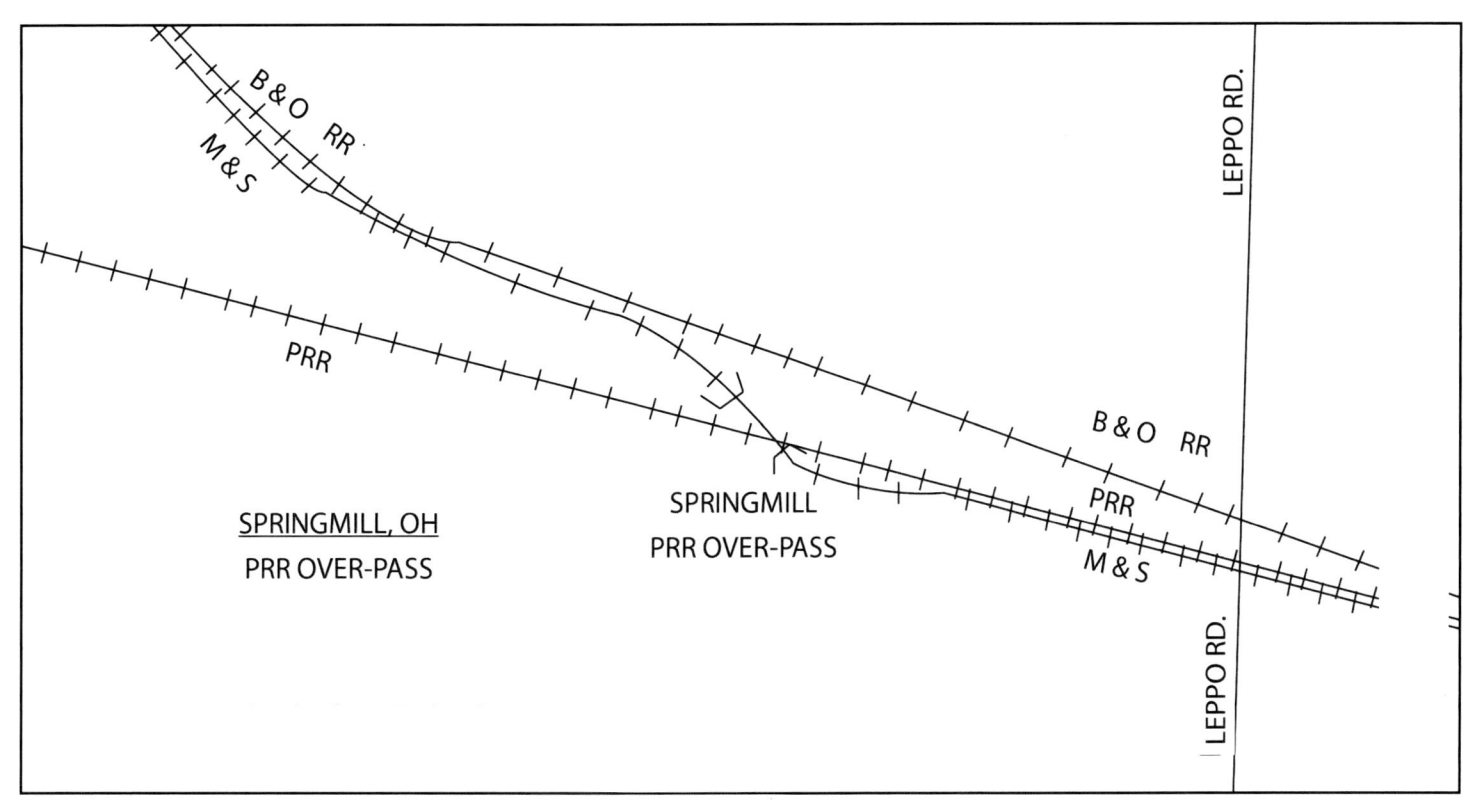

The M&S went over a high bridge over the Pennsylvania Railroad just west of Leppo Road, as shown above.

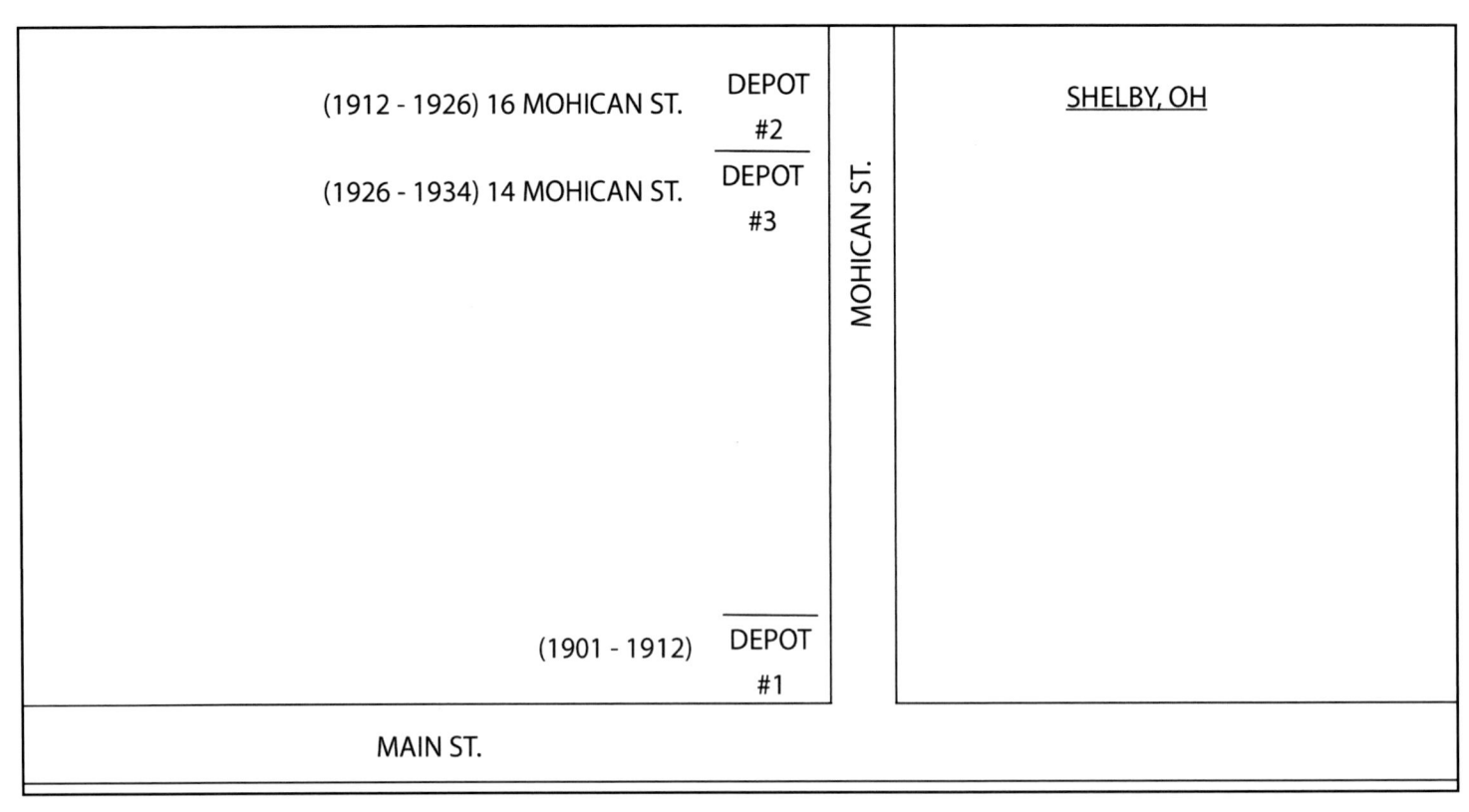

```
|                                    | DEPOT |           | SHELBY, OH |
| (1912 - 1926) 16 MOHICAN ST.       |  #2   |           |            |
|                                    |-------|           |            |
| (1926 - 1934) 14 MOHICAN ST.       | DEPOT |MOHICAN ST.|            |
|                                    |  #3   |           |            |
|                                    |       |           |            |
|                                    |-------|           |            |
| (1901 - 1912)                      | DEPOT |           |            |
|                                    |  #1   |           |            |
```

MAIN ST.

The interurban depot in Shelby changed locations 3 times from 1901 to 1934. The original depot, #1, was on the northwest corner of Main Street and Mohican Street. That was a rented affair and so in November 1912 the M&S opened their own depot at location #2 which was 16 Mohican Street. Effective December 1, 1926 the depot was again moved to #3, which was 14 Mohican Street. No tickets nor freight were handled from #3; it was simply a rented waiting room.

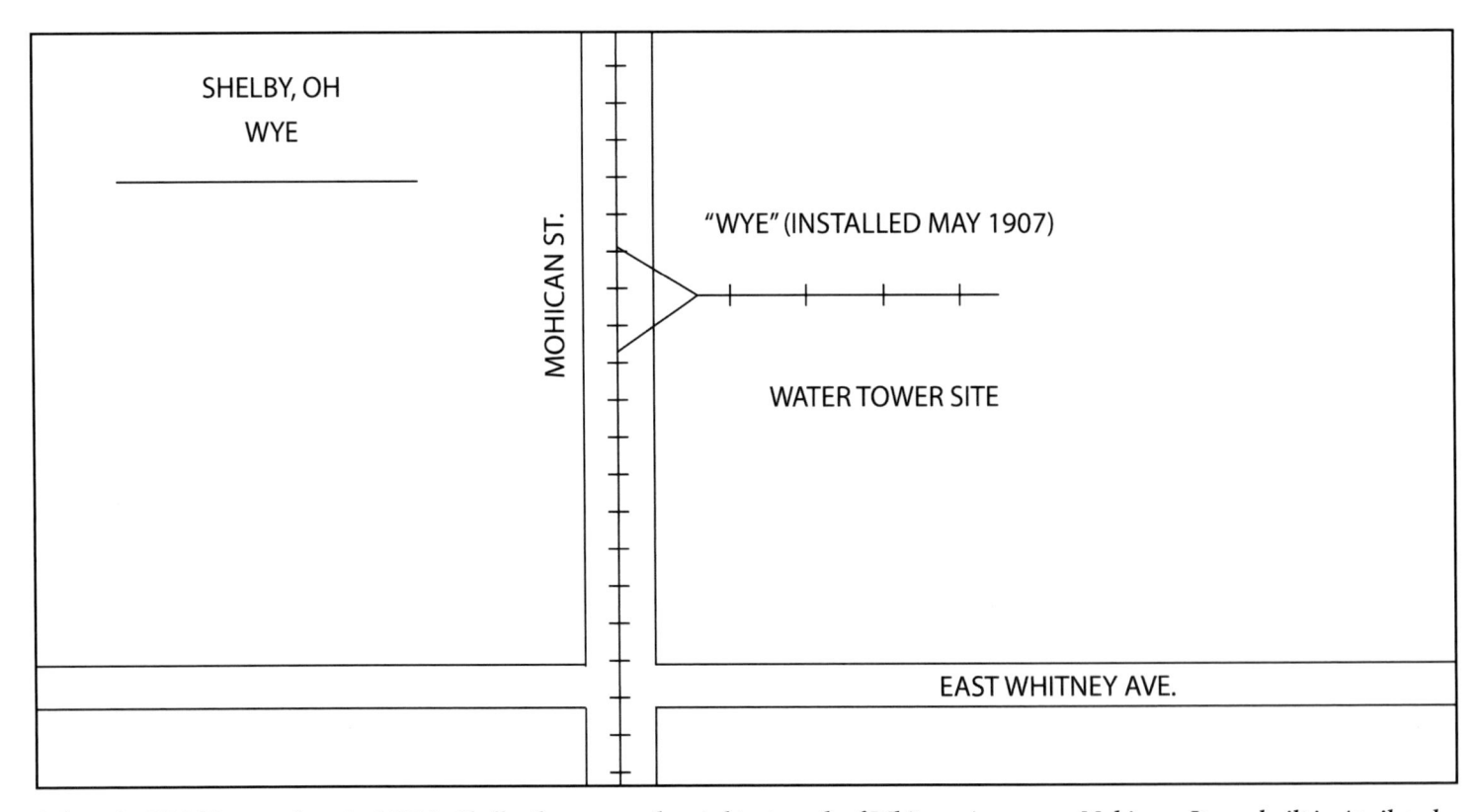

SHELBY, OH
WYE

MOHICAN ST.

"WYE" (INSTALLED MAY 1907)

WATER TOWER SITE

EAST WHITNEY AVE.

When the SN&M came along in 1907 in Shelby the wye was located just north of Whitney Avenue on Mohican. It was built in April and first used in early May.

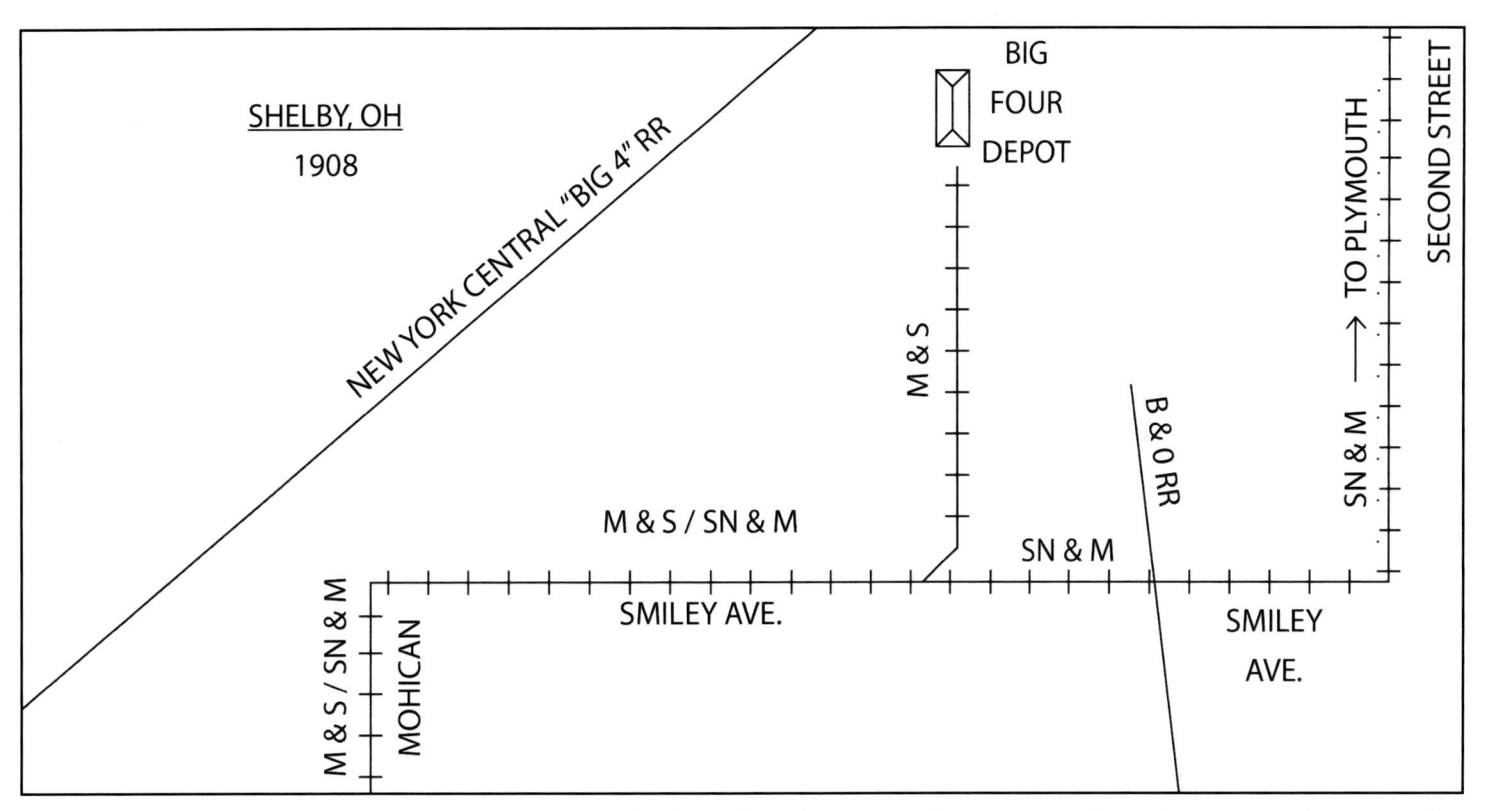

Streetcars and Interurbans of Richland County, Ohio

In Shelby the M&S turned east on Smiley and then immediately north to the Big Four depot. In 1907 the SN&M came south on Second, turned west on Smiley, and connected to the M&S just west of the B&O crossing. Joint-trackage was used from that point down to the interurban depot.

PART II
THE SANDUSKY, NORWALK, AND MANSFIELD ELECTRIC RAILWAY COMPANY

SANDUSKY, NORWALK & MANSFIELD ELECTRIC RAILWAY.

The Sandusky, Norwalk, and Mansfield Electric Railway was the 3rd interurban line to operate in Richland County, Ohio. It was in existence and operation originally having ended in Plymouth, reaching that city on July 1, 1905. It wasn't until April 4, 1907, that operations reached Shelby. At any rate, it ranks as one of the weakest interurbans in the United States. At its fullest it operated from Norwalk to Shelby with a branch over to Chicago Junction which later became Willard. The name was a misnomer as the line never operated to Sandusky nor to Mansfield. To reach either city passengers had to make connections either to the Lake Shore Electric at Norwalk or to the Mansfield and Shelby Electric Railway at Shelby. The purpose was "pie in the sky" at best as it tried to make important an interurban route from Mansfield through to Sandusky and even more so a "Lake to River" dream interurban. The promoters thought a combination of interurban lines from Portsmouth or Cincinnati to Sandusky would someday prove fruitful. It never did. The SN&M was one of the shortest-lived interurbans in the country, lasting only until March 25, 1921, due to the sparsely populated areas it served.

However, it must be understood that the SN&M was or could be a useful tool to other, bigger companies. During its life it was in constant interplay with the Lake Shore Electric Railway, the Cleveland Southwestern and Columbus Railway, the Mansfield & Shelby Electric Railway, and the Wheeling & Lake Erie Railroad in Norwalk, as will be described.

The Buckeye Traction Company

The beginning of the SN&M cannot be told without brief mention of the Buckeye Traction Company. In the years 1899-1900, Ohio seemed to have an interurban "craze" where many promoters and capitalists were going to build lines just about everywhere. Smooth-talking businessmen would often sway investors to invest in their proposed road. Many proposed lines were not successful and never laid rail, much less operated an interurban line. The Buckeye Traction Company never laid a rail either but it played a very important part in the SN&M's history. It was incorporated on January 3, 1901, and was projected to run, more or less, from Bucyrus to Norwalk. Route proposals changed over the next 2 years but ultimately it was decided to run from Bucyrus to New Washington, over to Plymouth and north to Steuben. At Steuben it would turn east to North Fairfield and then north to Norwalk. Through a complicated series of events, franchises were granted in Crawford and Huron Counties and a franchise was also eventually granted in Norwalk. Attorney Sherman Culp of Norwalk, B. B. Avery of Cleveland, and S. S. Burtsfield of Toledo would become the key officers of the route. By March 18, 1904, all of the right-of-way had been obtained and things were ready to go. In a strange twist of events, however, the Plymouth-Bucyrus section was dropped in favor of a future Plymouth-Shelby extension to meet the M&S in Shelby.

The Sandusky, Norwalk, and Mansfield

To add even more confusion on June 1, 1904, the Sandusky, Norwalk, and Mansfield Electric Railway was incorporated at a capital stock of $600,000. The incorporators were B. B. Avery of Cleveland, S. S. Burtsfield of Toledo, Sherman Culp of Norwalk, Leander Cole of Toledo, and Charles F. Milroy of Toledo. It can be recalled that Avery, Burtsfield, and Culp were officers of the Buckeye Traction Company. Since at this point it seemed a formality that the SN&M would simply build on the Buckeye Traction Company property, the deeds were merely transferred on June 13, 1904. And this is how the SN&M was born out of the Buckeye Traction Company.

The Beginning

The line was designed to operate south out of Norwalk to North Fairfield. North Fairfield was popular with the SN&M right from the beginning because citizens in that area purchased $400,000 of the stock. Since the right-of-way had been obtained construction began on June 13, 1904, at a location known as Beer's Corners south of Norwalk the same day that the deeds of the Buckeye Traction had been transferred. This would be the intersection of South Norwalk Road and Ridge Road. The line followed the west side of New State Road to North Fairfield. Construction was relatively slow but it is said that the Lake Shore Electric was loaning equipment and even men to help construct the line.

For the remainder of 1904, for the most part only grading and construction was taking place. By January 12, 1905, things had progressed quite nicely. The abutments over the stream north of New Haven had been completed and the steel bridge to go over had been delivered to the site. The grading from Newman's Corners (today's Rt. 103 and 598) west to Chicago Junction (later Willard) had been completed to the corporation limits. No track laying had taken place, however. The good news was that all of the grading had been completed from Norwalk south to North Fairfield, west to Steuben, and south to New Haven. S. S. Burtsfield became the president of the SN&M while Sherman Culp became vice-president.

First Car Arrives - Equipment

Construction continued during the spring and summer and by June 27, 1905, the road had reached Plymouth. The ultimate goal was to reach Shelby but as luck would have it that wouldn't occur for another 2 years. The big event of June 1905 was the arrival of the first car. The company originally put on order five combination passenger/freight coaches to the Niles Car Company in Niles, Ohio. The cars would be numbered 1-5 and for some reason car #3 arrived first. The car order changed a bit as will be explained later. At any rate, on June 30, 1905, car #3 arrived at the Lake Shore Electric shops in Sandusky where it would be fitted with the motors. After the car was fitted with the motors it was time to head to Norwalk. The car departed at 5:45 PM and went east on the Lake Shore Electric to Ceylon where it then came southwest on the LSE Southern Division to Norwalk, arriving at 7:00 PM. Norwalk citizens marveled at the sight and were very excited. Car #1 arrived at the Sandusky shops on July 2 and arrived in Norwalk at 9:00 PM that night.

It would take some more time before the remaining cars could be delivered. The combination passenger/freight coaches were 45 feet long and painted olive green with yellow trimmings. The cars had 16 seats in the main coach compartment and 4 seats in the rear smoking compartment. The baggage room and motorman area were in the same space. The seats were upholstered in green leather. Mechanically speaking the cars were fitted with four 50 horsepower motors built by the Bullock Electric Company of Cincinnati. These motors were geared for 45 mph. The trucks were built by Peckham Manufacturing of Kingston, NY. The cars each cost $3,000. Four of these coaches would be used on the SN&M until the end of operations in 1921.

Crossing Trouble at Newman

Meanwhile during 1905 there was some serious trouble with the crossing at Newman with the Baltimore & Ohio Railroad. The SN&M wanted to cross the tracks at grade level next to Peru Center Road. The B&O would hear none of that and was bound and determined to block the interurban from crossing their tracks at this location. Back on January 19, 1905, the Akron and Chicago Junction Division of the B&O filed an injunction against the SN&M and Judge Widman of Huron County granted that injunction. The SN&M made a plea to remove the injunction on May 25, but Judge Widman denied that plea. So the SN&M still could not cross at grade. This is where the real story begins.

The saga of Newman's Crossing would last over a year before a deal was reached satisfying both the SN&M and the B&O. Opening day for the SN&M to the public was slated for July 4, 1905. Growing suspicious of the SN&M, the B&O placed guards on duty at night in case the SN&M attempted to make a grade crossing. The matter landed in court once again. On June 22, 1905, the court hired a consultant by the name of Laylin to weigh in on the matter. Laylin recommended that a temporary grade crossing be allowed but ultimately an overhead bridge would need to be built. He also recommended that the SN&M have until at least June 1, 1906. Swayed by the consultant, Judge Widman then went ahead and granted the SN&M the authority to put in the temporary grade crossing. But the B&O wasn't done with its antics. On June 29, 1905, they began building a side track right at the site where the temporary crossing would be located. The SN&M of course asked the court for help but these things took time. On July 1, 1905, when car #3 on a trial run made it to Newman's, to circumvent the B&O's tactics the SN&M laid wooden rails over the B&O tracks right in the middle of Peru Center Road. The B&O tried to protest but Sheriff Snyder talked some sense into the B&O crew. When all was said and done, a B&O steam engine was sent to help the car across the wooden rails. The wooden rail scheme was used only for that day since the SN&M's next car would be arriving the following day. Because there was no permanent grade crossing yet, a car running south out of Norwalk would stop at Newman's. From there, passengers would get off that car and walk across the B&O tracks to a waiting car on the south side of the B&O (and vice versa). This meant one of the SN&M coaches would work "the north side" and the other coach "the south side." Later a walking platform was constructed until the fiasco could be resolved.

On July 19, 1905, the crossing diamonds were finally dropped off at the site to be installed. The next day when the SN&M crews came by they noticed that they were gone. Obviously suspecting the B&O, the law was called upon and the next day the diamonds magically reappeared. Finally, on July 24, 1905, a Judge Suhr granted the SN&M the authority to install the crossing but they had a sheriff stand by in case the B&O caused any trouble. In a never ending quest to cause problems for the poor SN&M, the B&O dumped ballast and parked gondolas on their tracks right in the way of the crossing. The SN&M called upon the sheriff and the following day of course the gondolas were gone and the ballast cleaned up. The B&O filed another injunction on July 26 and on August 7 it was heard in court. This time the judge allowed the temporary crossing but ordered the SN&M to build the overpass by the stated June 1, 1906, recommendation by Laylin. However, that would at least eliminate the two-car arrangement on each side of the B&O at Newman's. It took until February 16, 1906, for the bridge plans to be approved by the SN&M and the B&O and until April 12, 1906, for construction to begin. It was completed and opened on July 28, 1906, well past the due date but owing to the fact that progress was being made the courts (and the B&O) were forgiving. It is said that the SN&M and B&O were to both bear some percentage of the cost of the bridge but those numbers are not known. According to the SN&M company files, the bridge over the B&O here was Bridge #17. It was one steel pony pin connected truss bridge, 66 ½ feet long and 6'9" wide. It had 2 concrete piers with piling and tressel timbers. There was earthen filling for north and south approaches to the overhead crossing. The bridge height was 21 feet above the B&O rails and the total cost of the bridge was estimated to be $18,000. The court ordered the B&O pay $5,000 of that, but of course the SN&M had to maintain the bridge.

To make matters worse, back on September 27, 1905, a passenger by the name of Ruthie Clapp was a passenger on one of the cars. At Newman's she had to alight from the car to walk across the B&O to get on the waiting car on the other side of the tracks. When she was stepping down from the car she fell and hurt her leg. She had medical expenses and so sued the SN&M for $5,000. This suit was later reduced to $2,000. The lawsuit lasted for over two years because the SN&M contested it heavily.

The overhead bridge at Newman shortly after it was completed in 1906. This view is looking west down the Baltimore and Ohio Tracks. The bridge was 66 ½ feet long, 6'9" wide, and 21 feet high. (Willard Library)

Opening Day

On Saturday July 1, 1905, car #3 left Norwalk southbound at 10:25 AM and arrived at North Fairfield at 11:00 AM. The crew was motorman James Trimmer and Conductor Thomas. The first paying customer on the SN&M was C. E. Baker of Townsend. The other passengers were Sherman Culp and son Henry, A. E. Hill of Monroeville, and Sheriff Snyder in case there was trouble at Newman's. Snyder had injunction papers against the B&O signed by Judge Charles Suhr the previous evening. A large crowd in downtown Norwalk saw the car off and crowds lined Norwood Avenue and cheered. It appears the car ran all the way to Plymouth after going across the temporary crossing at Newman's and waiting for the overhead wire to be finished into Plymouth ahead of it. It must have been quite awhile because it was reported the car didn't make it into Plymouth until near midnight. According to reports on July 2, car #3 made many runs to and from the B&O at Newman's. It was very slow going from Plymouth to Newman's because there was no wye track on the SN&M yet on which to turn cars around. The motors in forward were geared for 45 mph, but reverse was much slower, near 10 mph.

On July 2, at 9:00 PM, car #1 arrived in Norwalk from the LSE Sandusky shops and was placed on the LSE siding. The equipment roster and operations at this point is a bit of a mystery at times. On July 3 there were two cars operating (#3 and #1) and it is thought that #3 worked the south end or south side of Newman's and #1 worked the north end while the crossing saga was going on at Newman's as already mentioned. This situation continued for quite some time because the third car, #4, didn't arrive in Norwalk after having been fitted at the LSE's Sandusky shops until August 25, 1905. Shortly thereafter the remaining two cars were to arrive, #2 and #5.

In addition to the passenger coaches, the SN&M built what was called a work motor which was simply a box for a cab on a flat car that was motorized. This was car #41 and was affectionately known as the *Mary Ann*. In the winter this was fitted with a snow plow. The SN&M also had 3 handcars and some gondola cars and dump cars for ballast. It was the *Mary Ann* that would pull around the gondolas and dump cars filled with rocks used to ballast the right-of-way.

On one of the first days of operation an SN&M car runs along Norwalk Road, later New State Road, just south of the intersection with Dublin Road. The right-of-way has no ballast yet as early operations were primeval. (Dennis Lamont)

Mystery Surrounds Car #2

After car #4 arrived on August 25, 1905, the SN&M was operating with 3 combination passenger/freight coaches from Niles, #1, #3, and #4. The other two hadn't arrived yet and not much is known about either. Car #2 appears to have arrived next, sometime after the arrival of #4. It was indeed exactly like the other combination cars but early photos show a #10 and a #2 painted on the car. It is not known why the car also had a #10, but it seems to have only lasted a short while.

The Mysterious Freight Motor

Early reports indicate that the SN&M had a dedicated freight motor. It was sometimes referred to as the baggage car. Since #5 had not shown up yet and the SN&M only ever used #1-#4 for passenger service, it is likely #5 was the freight motor. It doesn't appear to have arrived early like the other cars. On April 16, 1908, it was reported that the SN&M was to start a dedicated freight service. A dedicated freight car was being fitted with motors and would soon be in operation after that date and would make two trips per day between Mansfield and Sandusky carrying freight. On May 7, 1908, the freight motor had been fitted with the motors and was being painted in the North Fairfield car barn which had a small car repair and painting facility. It is known that this freight motor did indeed make some of these freight runs but it isn't known why or what type of freight was being handled.

Downtown Norwalk sometime after 1905. The Lake Shore Electric and SN&M depot were on the right at 12 East Main Street while the Cleveland Southwestern was across the street at 11 East Main. Until the SN&M moved to Benedict Avenue this location was always bustling with interurban cars and passengers. The SN&M began in Norwalk. (John Rehor)

The mysterious freight motor on the left has derailed on Benedict Avenue in 1910, at the intersection of Norwood. The work car or work motor, the Mary Ann, #41, is coming to the rescue. (Firelands Museum)

The mysterious car #2 that arrived after cars #3, #1, and #4, shown in Chicago Junction. It also has a #10. (Willard Library)

The Gravel Pit

North of North Fairfield, just south of Hanville Corners Road on the west side of Peru Center Road was the gravel pit for the SN&M. It was located on the farm of Elmer Burras. They had purchased this land as a source of stone to fill in and ballast the right-of-way. At first a simple switch and side track was extended westward into the pit. There was an overhead bridge over the pit track where wagons of stone could be dumped into the gondolas and dump cars sitting below the bridge. The *Mary Ann* would shove the cars back onto the pit track from the mainline for loading. The pit track was not electrified so the *Mary Ann* could not pull all the way into the pit. This was a very laborious operation. Men would shovel stone into wagons around the gravel pit. Teams of horses would then pull the wagon onto the overhead bridge and the stone would then either be dumped or shoveled down into the gondolas or dump cars. Once the cars were full, the *Mary Ann* would take them out onto the mainline to ballast the tracks. Ballasting the line this way took many months, and on opening day most of the line had no ballast.

The gravel pit was located on the Burras farm north of North Fairfield just south of Hanville Corners Road. Shown here is the spur track running underneath the overhead "dump" bridge with teams working the pit. (Dennis Lamont)

The Power and Power Equipment

During the month of June of 1905, most of the installation of the power equipment took place. The Lake Shore Electric was very heavily involved with the start up of the SN&M. In addition to fitting the cars in their Sandusky shops, the LSE is said to have loaned men and construction equipment to help the SN&M. They also supplied the SN&M with all of their power. A high tension AC (alternating current) line was constructed from the LSE's substation at Monroeville over to Beer's Corners south of Norwalk to meet the SN&M. Monroeville was a 15,000 V facility. From there this high tension line stayed more or less with the SN&M right-of-way. The line went down to North Fairfield where the SN&M was constructing a big passenger depot, waiting room, and ticket office. Behind this passenger depot, on the northwest corner of the square, was the substation. In 1903, the North Fairfield Hotel had been demolished to make room for the depot and substation. The equipment was installed by Wesly Ritter and William J. Wilkinson under the supervision of Mr. Toutman of the Bullock Electric Company of Cincinnati. Here, the AC was converted to DC and then sent out on a feeder wire in each direction on the SN&M to supply the trolley wire with 600 V DC. DC electricity, however, was only effective for about 12 miles. Knowing this the SN&M realized they'd need another substation at the other end of the line to insure enough power. On June 1,

Interior of the North Fairfield substation with operator Will Wilkinson. An extra generator was installed about 1908 so that the SN&M could also sell power commercially to North Fairfield businesses and later, residents. (Dennis Lamont)

1905, construction of a substation in Plymouth was started. By opening day it had been completed, and again the AC from the high tension line was converted to 600 V DC there and fed north. Later when the Shelby extension was completed the Plymouth substation fed the wire both directions. Although the equipment in the Plymouth substation wasn't exactly as that at North Fairfield, it was very similar. Cars theoretically then had enough power to operate the entire line. The poles along the right-of-way were made of chestnut wood and the ties were a mixture of woods.

Operations overall were fairly piecemeal at the beginning. Aside from the "gap" at Newman's until a crossing could be put into place, the SN&M had a fair amount of trouble getting into Chicago Junction on the "spur" from Newman's where a switch was put into place to connect to the line that would run over to that city. This switch was located just south of today's Rt. 103 along Rt. 598. After battling city council and even Huron County during the spring, the first car finally arrived in Chicago Junction at the corner of Myrtle Avenue and Pearl at the Scheidley Hotel on August 31, 1905. The depot for the SN&M would be located in a ramshackle building on the southwest corner of that intersection for a number of years. From July 3 to August 31, the Chicago Junction car operated to various other "terminals" between Newman and Chicago Junction. Since the SN&M only had 2 cars until August 25, until then car #3 ran the stretch between Plymouth and Newman's, and Newman's and Chicago Junction. Occasionally the Lake Shore Electric would loan them a car if passenger equipment was scarce and that was typically their Brill car, #60.

The area citizens were so excited about the interurban running through their communities it must be mentioned that two individuals south of Steuben at the intersection of Peru Center Road and Maple Ridge Road built their own little waiting station that was completed on or about August 31, 1905. It was built by Frank Campbell and A. F. Sweetland and the building measured 8 x 1 ft. While not an official "station" it was still known as Maple Ridge. The big event during this time frame was the arrival and operation of car #4 on August 25. The other two cars were to come a few weeks later so it appeared as though the SN&M had all of the necessary equipment to provide good service.

First Schedule

Even though the line wasn't completed all the way into Chicago Junction yet, the first passenger schedule was issued on July 13, 1905. Cars rolled south out of Norwalk on a basic "3-hourly schedule." However there was an early car that left North Fairfield at 6:15 AM and ran north to Norwalk probably just to get the car to Norwalk since no dedicated car barn had been built yet. Cars then left Norwalk at 7:00 AM, 10:00 AM, 1:00 PM, 4:00 PM, and 7:00 PM. These cars were all for Plymouth. At the other end of the line, Plymouth, the schedule was slightly different. Cars rolled north at 7:00 AM, 11:00 AM, 2:00 PM, 5:00 PM, 7:00 PM, and 11:00 PM. That 11:00 PM car did not go all the way back to Norwalk but terminated in North Fairfield instead (because there was no storage spot in Norwalk). Chicago Junction had a schedule as well. Cars rolled east for Norwalk at 8:00 AM, 11:00 AM, 2:00 PM, 5:00 PM, 8:00 PM and 11:00 PM. From Chicago Junction to Plymouth: 9:00 AM, 12:00 PM, 3:00 PM, 6:00 PM, 9:00 PM, and midnight. It is possible this schedule was confusing to passengers but basically it was the car arriving in one city, waiting, then going back. If a passenger rode one-way from Norwalk to Plymouth it cost 50 cents and to Chicago Junction 45 cents and vice versa. From Chicago Junction to Plymouth was only 15 cents. This early schedule was also set up to meet Lake Shore cars in Norwalk with a minimum amount of waiting. Also of importance is the fact that when this schedule was released "Chicago Junction" wasn't in the village; it was only to Bender's Corners which is today's Rt. 99/Rt. 103 intersection. As previously mentioned the village wasn't reached until August 31.

A Quick Tour

Cars left Norwalk from the depot at 12 East Main Street which was shared with the Lake Shore

Electric. Running west the line turned south onto Benedict Avenue and went down Benedict Hill. The line was in the street down Norwood moving to the west side of the road at the city limits. At this point the road became Ridge Road. At Beer's Corners where New State Road peels off the interurban swung over and joined the west side of New State Road to North Fairfield. At the city limits the line went into the middle of the street. The North Fairfield depot was still under construction at this point but passengers could get on and off cars here on the northwest corner of the square. Heading west in the street the line aimed for Steuben on Rt. 162. At the western city limits the line went to the south side of the road. The car barn would be located here and was still under construction. Rolling west the line followed the south side of Rt. 162 to a point just east of Rt. 61. From there the line in a sweeping arc ran northwest to join the old Clinton Air Line Railroad bed. This railroad bed was constructed in 1853-1856, and was part of a plan to construct an "air line railroad" from Buffalo to Chicago. Money ran out and another route was chosen; much of the roadbed was built but rails were never laid. The roadbed was ideal here for the SN&M because the fill was already constructed at the Huron River. Running west then on this road bed the north side of Steuben was reached. Behind the school the line then aimed southwest on a 45 degree angle reaching Rt. 162 where a siding and depot was later located. Continuing on, the SN&M crossed Peru Center Road and then joined the west side. At Maple Ridge Road, where the little waiting room was constructed, the line went back over to the east side of the road. Following the road the B&O was finally reached. Prior to the overhead bridge being constructed, passengers had to get off the car on the north side of the B&O and walk across to a waiting car on the south side. Continuing south and after crossing Rt. 103, Newman's was reached. A passenger could get off the car here and ride the "spur car" over to Chicago Junction or stay on the car and continue to Plymouth. Heading south to Plymouth the line stayed on the east side of the road. The SN&M interurban depot at New Haven was located in a store front affair slightly opposite the Odd Fellow's Hall on the west side of Route 61 just north of Prairie Street. This was the ticket office and after November of 1907 the joint passenger-Wells Fargo Express office. Because the track was on the opposite side of the road of the depot, a freight shed was built on the east side of the road in the lot north of the Odd Fellow's Hall. Both the store building and the freight shed had the distinct Wells Fargo and Express "diamond" symbol displayed after 1907. The line crossed Rt. 224 and just south of Skinner Road the line swerved over to the west side of the road. Again the line joined the middle of the street at the city limits of Plymouth and ran down to the southern terminal of the line at the Smith Hotel. That's as far as the line went at this point. The Shelby extension was coming but wouldn't be completed for another two years. The spur car for Chicago Junction simply ran on the south side of Rt. 103 all the way past the B&O overpass where it then ran in the middle of the street. The line turned north on Myrtle Avenue and ended at Pearl. The depot was located in the Williams Building on the southwest corner. Later the "spur car" had another trolley pole added to the top so that the conductor didn't have to swing the other pole around to back the car in or out. The line was extended north, but that will be discussed later.

The other annoyance of the early operations was that the big SN&M interurban cars were called "single-ended." This meant that they could only run in "forward" from one end. Some cars on other lines were "double-ended" meaning there were controllers at each end of the car and could be run in forward from either end. The motors on the cars were geared for 45 mph running forward. Running in reverse was much slower. The SN&M had no wye tracks anywhere on the system in the early part of operations so if a car ran forward to Plymouth, to get back to Newman's it had to run in reverse which was likely only 10 mph. The SN&M would

The interurban depot and waiting room at Plymouth was in the Smith Hotel "two doors north of the bank" on the square. In the above photo the sign is seen clearly on the right. The car is northbound. (Plymouth Area Historical Society)

The track originally ended at Plymouth. Construction to Shelby wouldn't begin until 1906, and wasn't opened until mid-1907. Shown here is a car at "line's end" at the square in Plymouth. (Timothy Brian McKee)

later put in wye tracks at various locations. This problem was never solved for the Chicago Junction car. That car always had to run in reverse either into or out of Chicago Junction and was quite annoying to passengers.

The Plymouth and Shelby Traction Company

Finally the ball got rolling on the bigger improvements that the SN&M badly needed. Funds had dried up when the right-of-way was constructed to Plymouth. The goal all along was to reach Shelby to connect with the Mansfield & Shelby Electric Railway owned by the Mansfield Railway, Light & Power Company. There were no long-term business gains to simply terminate in Plymouth. A subsidiary was formed and incorporated on September 4, 1905, with fresh investment money. It was incorporated by SN&M officers B. B. Avery, G. L. Rebman, Sherman Culp, Frank L. Scott, and Sterling Parks at a capital of $200,000. It would be some time before construction could get under way, but it was a start. Property bought with the capital was used to secure right-of-way to Shelby. Even though this was essentially a subsidiary of the SN&M it always remained on the records as a separate property and was never included in the SN&M documents.

North Fairfield Improved

At North Fairfield things were moving along smoothly. A wye track was installed at the gravel pit on October 27, 1905. Although it wasn't exactly in an ideal location at least cars could turn around somewhere. Also in October of 1905, the depot at North Fairfield was completed. The structure was a very ornate stone block building which housed the ticket office, waiting room, and even a dispatcher's office later. The substation was located directly behind. The block used was from the Artificial Stone Company of Chicago Junction. In November a siding was installed at the west corporation line and a car barn constructed with the siding running through. This car barn would serve as a minor repair shop, painting facility, and storage for two cars. It had a concrete floor and foundations and a car pit. The siding was 375 feet long.

There were two other sidings in the North Fairfield area that were used heavily for loading and unloading. The first was one north of North Fairfield at the Ralph Hoyt farm and the other was west of the village at the Wilbur Hoyt farm. Livestock, crops, flax, and other commodities were loaded on these sidings.

The North Fairfield depot and substation was ornate. Why? Of the $600,000 issued in bonds for the SN&M, North Fairfield area residents bought up $400,000 of those, or 2/3. It was located on the northwest corner of the square. (Dennis Lamont)

Another view focuses on the substation which was immediately west of the waiting room. (Dennis Lamont)

A hot commodity in the North Fairfield area was flax. At the siding located north of North Fairfield piles of it wait to be loaded onto an SN&M car. (Dennis Lamont)

The original car barn at North Fairfield was at the western corporation limits. Shown here is an eastbound car coming off private right-of-way and entering the street at the car barn. (Dennis Lamont)

On to Shelby

Finally on April 9, 1906, work on the Shelby extension began outside of Plymouth. There was still some legal work to be done inside the Plymouth corporation limits so construction began this day at the south corporation line at the J. R. Channing farm. Grading began to the south by contractor Fox and a small team of men. As will be learned, there were two major lawsuits which held up the construction to Shelby, not to mention franchise issues with the Mansfield and Shelby Electric in Shelby. Therefore work progressed very slowly.

While nothing seemed to be getting done on the Plymouth and Shelby Traction section, the overhead bridge at Newman's was finally completed and opened on July 28, 1906. This was an operational relief to the SN&M because cars no longer had to wait on each other on each side of the tracks or wait on the B&O trains after the temporary crossing was installed.

Some minor trouble was encountered for the P&S in Plymouth on October 27, 1906. The interurban had constructed an at-grade crossing with the Northern Ohio Railroad on the south side of town in October. On the 27th however the Northern Ohio Railroad pulled up the crossing and also 40 feet of track on each side of the railroad. The SN&M took the Northern Ohio Railroad to court on October 29 and an agreement must have been reached because there was no further trouble. Bigger trouble had already started brewing north of Shelby. When the P&S decided to start buying property they planned to run along Rt. 61 in front of the James H. Dempsey farm. Dempsey did not approve and fought the P&S. It was one of the longest lasting court battles on the SN&M: It began on September 4, 1906, in probate court and after numerous hearings and appeals it wasn't settled until April 29, 1908, when the property was officially granted to the P&S. Although an injunction had been granted against Dempsey prior to that to allow cars to run into Shelby, it significantly delayed cars running through the property into Shelby.

A small battle ensued between the P&S and the Plymouth school board. The claim was that the tracks passing in front of the Kuhn School at Dininger Road would be hazardous and unsafe. Again, the matter was taken to court. In a bizarre court ruling on November 30, 1906, the P&S had to pay the school board $125 which would be used to move the school house farther to the west away from the track.

Construction continued slowly south to Shelby. On January 5, 1907, the grading reached the Shelby corporation limits. Unfortunately three things had yet to be accomplished. The first was an at-grade crossing with the New York Central's Big Four line on the north side of Shelby at Second Street and Elm Street. On East Smiley the B&O Railroad would have to be crossed and lastly a connection just west of the B&O on East Smiley would have to be made with the Mansfield & Shelby Electric Railway. These would prove to take some time to accomplish.

By February 18, 1907, the overhead wire had been completed all the way to M&S wires in Shelby but the track hadn't been completed. By April 4, 1907, the crossing over the Big Four had been completed but not the crossing over the B&O and the track did not connect to the M&S. However, service was started. On April 4, 1907, cars began running to Shelby from Plymouth but only to the corner of Second Street and Smiley Avenue. Regular service from this location however was pared back. On Sunday April 7, a schedule was instituted where cars would leave Shelby northbound at 8:00 AM and then every 2 hours after that until midnight. However that was Sunday only and the other days of the week the interurban did not operate. This didn't last long because on April 29, 1907, the B&O diamonds on East Smiley Avenue were completed and the tracks were connected with the M&S electric line. Therefore service could begin to the interurban depot on Mohican Street.

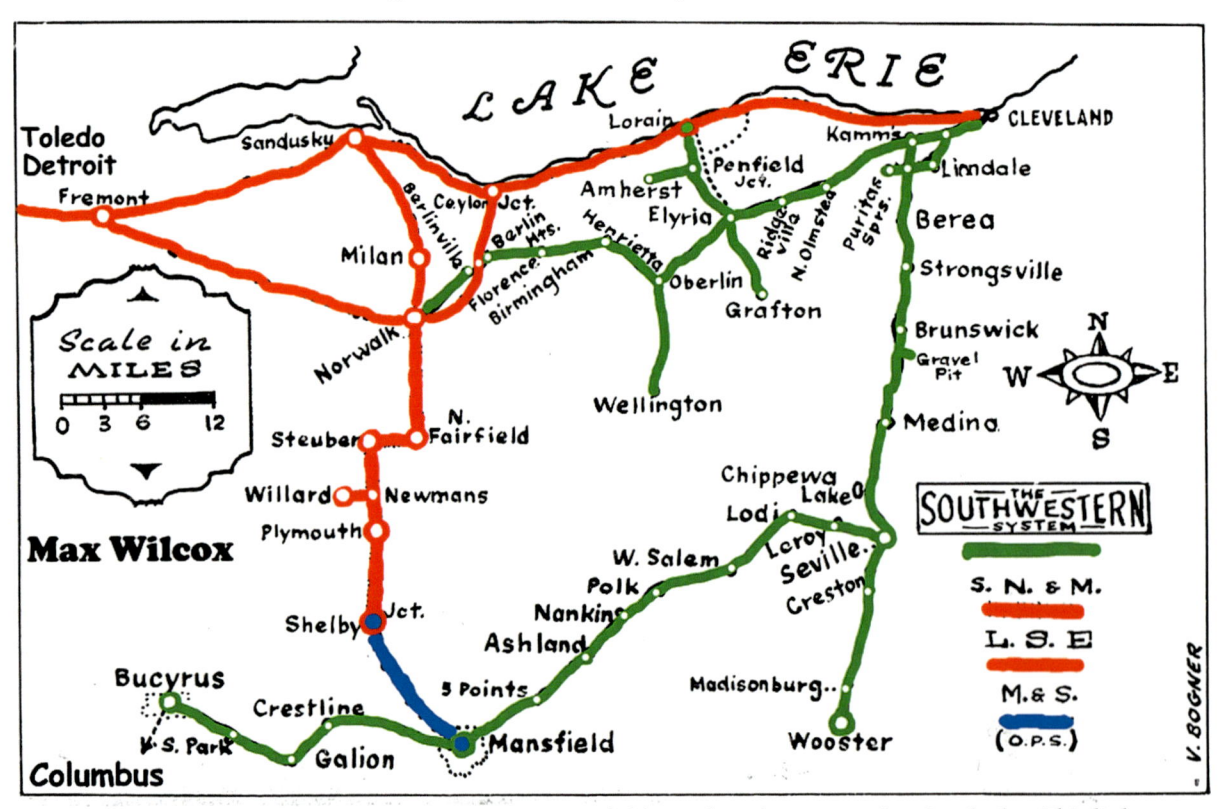

After the SN&M was completed to Shelby in 1907, Mansfield was directly connected to Sandusky. This link was thought to be part of a larger "Ohio River to Lake Erie" dream route. The M&S line above is shown in blue, the SN&M in red, and the Lake Shore Electric in orange from Norwalk to Sandusky. (Max Wilcox Collection)

Construction crews get underway on the square at Plymouth in October of 1906 for the Plymouth-Shelby extension. (Plymouth Area Historical Society)

Car #4 does the honors on the new Plymouth and Shelby extension through the square in Plymouth in 1907. (Plymouth Area Historical Society)

The Sutter Furniture Company sold the SN&M a strip of right-of-way on the east side of Mohican Street north of Whitney back on April 13 to construct a wye track. On May 3, 1907, the wye track was completed. Now the big SN&M interurban cars could turn around at Shelby and at the gravel pit at North Fairfield. A wye would be installed at Benedict and Main in Norwalk in late 1908 so shortly there would be wyes at both ends of the line. The next day, on May 4, 1907, the schedule was issued and now cars could operate the full length of the system. Cars left Shelby northbound for Norwalk starting at 6:55 AM and every 90 minutes thereafter until 11:45 PM. The last car ran only to Plymouth.

A Quick Tour From Plymouth to Shelby

Riding to Shelby was relatively simple. Cars rolled south on Plymouth Street, today's Rt. 61, all the way to the corporation limits on the south edge of town. At that point the track went to the west side of Rt. 61. There was a deviation just after passing Opdyke Road as the interurban had to "bow" around a big ravine. This was also the location of the big lake of the long-forgotten Huron Valley Park, which was sometimes referred to as the Huron Valley Amusement Park. South of the ravine the interurban rejoined the west side of Rt. 61. Approaching Hazel Brush road the interurban crossed to the east side of Rt. 61 a few hundred feet north of Hazelbrush. The line then followed the east side of Rt. 61 to a point just prior to reaching Bistline Road where it took off on private right-of-way. It went across the Black Fork and headed straight for the intersection of London West Road and North Broadway. Crossing London West Road at this point it picked up the east side of Broadway. The line ran down to Cline where it then arced to the southeast to pick up street running in the middle of Second Street Extension. The line crossed State Street and crossed the New York Central's Big Four line. The line continued to head straight south down the middle of Second Street. At East Smiley cars turned west. Ahead the B&O Railroad was crossed and immediately the switch with the Mansfield & Shelby interurban was reached, between the Spring Hinge and Brightman Manufacturing. From here the SN&M and M&S ran together turning south on Mohican Street. Just before East Whitney the cars pulled into the wye forward and then backed out the other end and ran in reverse to the Shelby interurban depot.

Plymouth was proud of the Shelby extension. This amazing right-of-way photo was taken south of the square immediately upon construction, looking north. (Plymouth Area Historical Society)

After the Shelby extension, or P&S section was completed, a northbound car from Shelby rounds the curve at the Rt. 61/Rt. 98 split and heads up Plymouth Street. (Plymouth Area Historical Society)

Cleveland Southwestern & Columbus Railway Company

In mid-1907, the Cleveland, Southwestern, and Columbus Railway Company took a controlling interest in the Mansfield Railway, Light & Power Company which controlled the streetcar system and the interurban line to Shelby. This was significant because this is the first time a relationship

Prior to the Cleveland Southwestern completing their line from Seville west to Mansfield, they used the SN&M to reach Mansfield and Bucyrus via Elyria and Norwalk. A stronger relationship was developed later. The photo shown here is on the north side of Plymouth where the track left the street. Immediately after leaving the street the "Plymouth siding" was reached. This is the Cleveland Southwestern's beautiful officials' car named The Josephine posing on the siding. (Shelby Museum of History, Willis McCaleb Collection)

was established between the SN&M and the CSW. On July 6, 1907, the Cleveland Southwestern purchased 5,025 shares of common stock of the MRL&P out of the 10,000 available thus giving the CSW a controlling interest. The CSW's route from Mansfield east to Seville had not been completed yet so there was no route to their Mansfield-Bucyrus line from Cleveland which had just been included in the CSW merger. Therefore the SN&M was the logical route to use. The CSW cars would run to Norwalk on their Cleveland-Norwalk "western" division. From there the SN&M would be taken south to Shelby. At Shelby the M&S was used to get to Mansfield and then the old Ohio Central Traction division west to Bucyrus. Even though the SN&M was still involved heavily with the LSE this relationship would have long-lasting effects on the SN&M.

First Cedar Point Trip

On August 7, 1906, the Lutheran Church put on an excursion to Cedar Point. Because the SN&M could run north to Norwalk and meet Lake Shore Electric cars to take them to the Sandusky Pier to meet a boat, they decided to take the "electric line." The SN&M's equipment was not sufficient so the Lake Shore Electric loaned them three of their cars which made the run. All area Lutheran Church members were welcome to board the cars and ride to Cedar Point. This relationship would continue for the 1908 and 1911 seasons as will be seen.

The track originally ended at Plymouth and wasn't extended south to Shelby until 1906-1907. Shown here is a trip for all area Lutheran Church members to Cedar Point. The SN&M's equipment was not sufficient to provide such a large excursion for the time so the Lake Shore Electric loaned them some cars. The date of the excursion was August 7, 1906. (Author)

First Fatality

On August 21, 1907, the SN&M had its first fatality. Mrs. Cornelia M. Andrews was visiting friends along the Fairfield Road south of Norwalk near Stop 8 and wished to board the southbound car. She flagged down the motorman who then gave a whistle blast to let her know that he would stop to allow her to board. Thinking it was okay she crossed the track in front of the car but the car had not slowed enough to stop in time. The car hit and killed Mrs. Andrews. The crew were motorman Drew Mickel and conductor Charles Stower. A lawsuit was later filed by the administrator of her estate, Carl F. Meade, in the amount of $10,000.

Wells Fargo Express horse and buggy. The SN&M contracted with and handled Wells Fargo Express shipments. (Dennis Lamont)

Wells Fargo Express Company

The SN&M officially entered the freight business on November 20, 1907, when it joined the Wells Fargo Express Company. Offices were located at Shelby, Plymouth, New Haven, Chicago Junction, Steuben, North Fairfield, and Norwalk. It must be explained that previously on December 27, 1906, the track in Chicago Junction was extended north past Maple Avenue to the Owens Store 3 buildings north of Maple. The Wells Fargo office was placed in the interurban depot on the southwest corner of Myrtle and Pearl in the Williams Building. It should also be mentioned that a depot was built in Steuben along with a siding on November 7, 1907. This would serve as the passenger and Wells Fargo depot. In addition to Wells Fargo the SN&M did carry other specialty freight. For example, Chicago Junction and later Willard did a thriving celery business.

Carts of celery were often loaded at the depot. North of North Fairfield was also prime flax territory. Piles of flax could be seen during harvest season along the interurban right-of-way. Even though the M&S line from Shelby to Mansfield didn't handle Wells Fargo because they were participating in the Electric Package Agency, some Wells Fargo freight could be forwarded from the SN&M to the M&S in Shelby if required, and the M&S would schedule a special freight run. It is important to note that mail was handled regularly. As mentioned in Part I, the Cleveland Southwestern had to use the SN&M route for Electric Package freight from Shelby to Norwalk until their line from Mansfield to Cleveland was completed in February of 1909.

It appears as though the combination passenger and freight cars, #1-#4, were handling most of the freight. The mysterious freight motor, however, comes back into question again because during this time reports of sporadic dedicated freight runs through from Mansfield to Sandusky were seen beginning in mid-1908. It is possible that #5 was making these runs as described earlier. In the spring of 1910, this freight motor was taken out of service. One report indicates that it had a propensity to derail. However, on November 3, 1910, the SN&M began running the freight motor between Mansfield and Sandusky. This could have been to handle the Wells Fargo freight that needed to be forwarded to Mansfield. It didn't last long, however. On December 28, 1910, the Guarantee Title and Trust Company of Cleveland hired a consultant to evaluate the SN&M due to financial losses and potential receivership. In that report the freight motor had no motor equipment to run. It was never heard from again and any Wells Fargo service from Shelby to Mansfield was handled by the M&S electric with their own equipment. The freight motor was sold to the Toledo, Port Clinton, and Lakeside Railway Company shortly after this report.

SN&M original depot at Steuben located just east of the main intersection. The Wells Fargo Express sign is visible on the right side of the depot porch roof. (Willard Library)

1908 – Big Progress And A Few Setbacks

On May 4, 1908, a "through-service" was instituted with the Lake Shore Electric, SN&M, and the

M&S lines. The service would be known as the Cedar Point Limited and was designed to be a fast, limited-stop service from Mansfield to Sandusky without changing cars. The trip would be limited to 8 stops total. The selling point to passengers is that this car would go directly to Cedar Point Pier at the foot of Columbus Avenue in Sandusky at Lake Erie. Passengers could then ride one of the boats over to Cedar Point. Schedules were synched up such that the limited car would meet the returning boat from Cedar Point at the pier.

The big news on May 7 was the story of the first limited run. It departed Mansfield at 7:30 AM and arrived in Norwalk at 8:58 AM. It stopped for two minutes in Norwalk and sped off to Sandusky. The crew was motorman James Trimmer and conductor A. C. Thomas. The impressive part was the run of 55 minutes from Shelby to Norwalk. Vice President Sherman Culp stated that the company would like to run two of these limited cars per day and they wished to maintain the 55 minute run time from Shelby to Norwalk. Only one car was put on the line and the schedule did not remain that ambitious. For example the southbound car schedule was as follows: depart Sandusky at 6:45 PM, Norwalk at 7:35 PM, and arrive in Shelby at 8:45 PM. This running schedule was easier to maintain and gave a 70-minute leeway between Norwalk and Shelby and a two-hour leeway between Sandusky and Shelby.

Lake Shore Electric car races northbound at an unknown location, but likely north of North Fairfield along Norwalk Road. The LSE motors were geared for 60 mph. This photo was taken on one of the 1908 summer runs to Cedar Point. (Dennis Lamont)

Sad news on the SN&M occurred on July 25, 1908. A young man by the name of Sherman Bodley who lived near Plymouth was killed on the SN&M track at a location known as Kuhn's Crossing between Shelby and Plymouth. Kuhn's Crossing was at the Rt. 61-Dininger Road intersection and was named after the Kuhn School which sat on the southwest corner of the intersection. As mentioned before, prior to the CSW being completed from Seville to Mansfield, the CSW used the SN&M as part of their Cleveland-Mansfield route. CSW car #129 was heading northbound at this point as an "extra" and was not the regular car and was not on the schedule. It is thought that when Bodley saw the car he may have fouled the right-of-way trying to flag the car but this car was not supposed to stop so it did not slow down. Ironically CSW #129 had been in a runaway wreck in Mansfield just the day before. As if this wasn't tragic enough, the 22 year-old left behind a wife and two children with the youngest being two weeks old.

Plymouth Wreck

The biggest public setback, however, was yet to come. On August 28, 1908, the first northbound car out of Plymouth that departed at 6:30 AM rounded the little curve in the track just north of the corporation line. The car was in the charge of motorman J. C. Clutter and as he rounded this little curve he saw another car coming at him on the same track. The southbound car was in the charge of motorman Henry Dildine. Clutter and Dildine both attempted to stop their cars but realizing it was too late the motors were thrown in reverse and both jumped before impact. The cars came together with enough impact to smash in the front of both cars. The passengers in each car, having sensed impending peril, ran to the back of the car. Miraculously the cars had slowed enough that only two passengers were injured: Mrs. Earl Plummer of Plymouth and an unnamed section hand riding on one of the cars.

Plymouth wreck of August 28, 1908. Car #4 is on the left with #2 in the middle. Car #3 came to the rescue. (Plymouth Area Historical Society)

Plymouth wreck of August 28, 1908. Car #4 is on the left with #2 in the middle. Car #3 came to the rescue. (Plymouth Area Historical Society)

Smashup at Plymouth on August 28, 1908. (Plymouth Area Historical Society)

A further explanation was given by the company after the wreck. The northbound car was #4 and the southbound car was #2. The little curve was known as Hamilton's Curve and there was a siding just south of there known as Plymouth Siding which was 230 feet long. One of the cars was supposed to wait on the other and each of the crews misunderstood. No further details were provided but an investigation was done by the SN&M.

On Labor Day of 1908 (September 7), the last Lake Shore Electric limited to Cedar Point ran for the season. It is said that many enjoyed it and it was hoped that it would be run again next summer.

In North Fairfield during 1908, a 10-horsepower motor was installed in the substation so that electricity could be sold to North Fairfield residents. Originally it was sold to businesses on the square but now more could be sold with this additional motor.

Front end of car #2 after the Plymouth collision on August 28, 1908. This photo is at an unknown location as the two cars involved in the wreck had been towed to a siding to await transport for repairs. (Plymouth Area Historical Society)

Front end of car #4 after the Plymouth collision on August 28, 1908. This photo is at an unknown location as the two cars involved in the wreck had been towed to a siding to await transport for repairs. (Plymouth Area Historical Society)

Ownership Change – 1909

The big news of 1909 came fairly early in the year. On or about January 5, 1909, two individuals purchased outright the SN&M. G. A. Bartholomew of Cleveland and Mrs. Annie Stentz of Monroeville purchased the interurban line by purchasing all of the stock. Stentz had been purchasing the stocks throughout December of 1908. It is likely the purchase was made because the SN&M fit into some larger plan of a bigger interurban system that they had devised. At any rate S. S. Burtsfield retired as president. G. A. Bartholomew became president and general manager and Anna Stentz took over vice president from Sherman Culp. Culp seems to have disappeared from the SN&M in 1909, but would return. And as we shall see, this seems to be the first event that led to the eventual break with the Lake Shore Electric and the beginning of a new relationship with the Cleveland Southwestern.

An improvement, in late 1908, was made in Norwalk when a wye track was constructed with the Lake Shore Electric at the corner of Main Street and Benedict Avenue. Previously there was simply a switch. SN&M cars could then turn around up at that intersection. Previously they had to turn on the gravel pit wye at North Fairfield and back to Norwalk. Also of note was the SN&M moving out of the waiting room with the Lake Shore Electric at Norwalk and establishing their own ticket office and waiting room. The announcement was made on March 25, 1909. The location at 46 Benedict Avenue was on the west side of the street just north of the Wheeling and Lake Erie depot and crossing. The SN&M also wanted to build a wye down there because the Lake Shore Electric was charging them 12 ½ cents per car to turn on the Main/Benedict wye. The SN&M was never able to get city council permission for the wye, however. The building was known as the Owens block and was built originally for the Sandusky Brewing Company. The first floor would be used as the waiting room, the second floor for general offices which were at this time in the Gardiner block in Norwalk, and the basement for a freight depot equipped with a motorized freight elevator. This also sort of severed the relationship the SN&M had with the LSE in Norwalk.

On April 24, 1909, the SN&M announced that they will build their own lines from both Shelby to Mansfield and from Norwalk to Sandusky. It had been stated by the company that they were dissatisfied with the track condition of the M&S line from Shelby to Norwalk and the right-of-way could not properly handle their heavier cars on potential "through-runs" from the two cities. The SN&M was also dissatisfied with the M&S schedule citing that passengers had to wait long periods of time in Shelby for an M&S car. This was likely a ploy to complete a full Mansfield-Sandusky line which would form a link in a larger "river to lake" line. Bartholomew wanted to extend his track south of the intersection of Second Street and East Smiley Avenue to Whitney Avenue. At Whitney Avenue the line would turn west and then south on Broadway. Running south on Broadway the line would run to a point south of Myers Road where it would then pick up the old Mansfield Short Line Railroad right-of-way to follow that into Mansfield. The MSL RR, a railroad grade with no rails ever being laid, was "constructed" by Charles French in the period 1898-1901 from Shelby to Mansfield. No rails were ever laid because funding dried up—if there ever even was funding. The roadbed remained and so it was prime for the SN&M to use. The MSL will be discussed in full in Part IV. Sherman Culp of the SN&M had already announced plans for the SN&M to run from Norwalk to Sandusky back in August 1907, and that route was going to go via Monroeville. None of this ever happened but it at least lent insight into the company's thinking.

The relationship with the LSE wasn't completely severed. The LSE was still selling them power after all. On July 1, 1909, a "through-service" with the LSE was again instituted but this wasn't a Cedar Point run. It was merely a service that ran from Shelby (instead of Mansfield) to Sandusky without change in Norwalk. The car left Shelby at 6:10 AM and every hour after that until 10:00 PM. The last car to leave Sandusky for Shelby was at 10:00 PM. It is not known who supplied the cars. The

M&S timed their schedule to meet these cars at Shelby. The service stopped on August 23, 1909, much earlier than the Lake Shore Electric Cedar Point limited had stopped the previous year.

In 1909, the SN&M moved out of the waiting room at Norwalk with the LSE and rented space at 46 Benedict Avenue to handle both passenger and freight. This photo is looking south on Benedict Avenue from Main. The car is pulling up for a station stop after having just crossed the Wheeling and Lake Erie Railroad. (Firelands Museum)

SN&M car #4 turns south onto Benedict Avenue from Main Street in Norwalk at the Glass Block Building. (Firelands Museum)

State of Affairs in 1909

What was the state of affairs of the SN&M in 1909? According to McGraw's, the SN&M had the following statistics published. There were 33 ½ miles of track which included the spur over to Chicago Junction. The 4 Niles combination passenger/freight coaches were listed along with 1 express or freight motor and 1 work car. Financially speaking things were not so good. At the end of 1907, the net deficit of the road was $8,604, and at the end of 1908, it was $19,474, a staggering increase. The 1908 statistic is despite having 345,655 revenue passengers for that year. The SN&M had $600,000 in bonds while the Plymouth and Shelby Traction was listed separately with $200,000. Sherman Culp had disappeared in 1909, after the Bartholomew/Stentz buyout and so the officers were listed as: G. A. Bartholomew president, general manager, and purchasing agent; A. M. Stentz, vice president; George S. Powley, secretary and treasurer; E. W. Frink, auditor and traffic manager; and A. J. Vickery, master mechanic.

A Snapshot in 1910

Despite the hype over the "through service" and Wells Fargo freight on the SN&M, it had been operating on a loss. Without going into the financial statistics, the picture was gloomy because the number of passengers was increasing over the years 1907-1909, but the net deficit in revenue was also increasing. On April 26, 1910, Mrs. Anna Stentz took over as president of the SN&M when G. A. Bartholomew retired. Immediately Mrs. Anna Stentz appointed Sherman Culp president while she took vice president, Culp's former position. Interestingly S. S. Burtsfield came back and was appointed general manager.

Another big event happened on April 29, 1910. The Cleveland Southwestern and Columbus Railway Company (CSW) purchased a very large block of stock of the SN&M that gave them control. The LSE over the years had toyed with the idea of purchasing the SN&M but never did. Even though the SN&M was operating at a loss the CSW thought they could make something useful of it. This seemed to be an intelligent purchase since the CSW already had a controlling interest in the Mansfield system and the M&S interurban. Since the LSE and CSW were fierce competitors this weakened the SN&M/LSE relationship even more. The officers after the purchase did not change.

On July 16, 1910, it was announced that the LSE would no longer be supplying power to the SN&M. The CSW was to supply the power from a small powerhouse in Norwalk located along the W&LE RR tracks just east of Benedict Avenue. The power plant was already in existence prior to the Cleveland Southwestern purchasing it to sell power. In 1903, the Northern Electric Company transferred the powerhouse to the Cleveland Southwestern Traction Company (it wasn't the Cleveland Southwestern and Columbus until April 30, 1907). It was likely at this time that the powerhouse name changed to Norwalk Gas and Electric because the Cleveland Southwestern Traction purchased that utility too. It was coal-fired but it also had a high-tension feeder from the CSW's big Elyria powerhouse. At any rate, the powerhouse from 1903 on was owned and operated by the interurban company and this is where the SN&M from 1910 until abandonment received their electricity.

There were two humorous lawsuits in 1910 against the SN&M that must be mentioned. An agreement within the franchise in Shelby stipulated that the SN&M had to help with paving a street should that street need to be improved. Second Street north of East Smiley needed to be paved and the city would do some percentage of the work while the SN&M was to do their stipulated share (unknown). When Shelby began paving Second Street the SN&M was nowhere to be found. Shelby City Council threatened to terminate the franchise and stop cars from running on September 21, 1910. After some legal wrangling the SN&M finally got to work. This was known locally as "The Second Street War" and raged into the summer of 1911. Later on November 26, 1910, the village of Plymouth sued the SN&M over an electrolysis issue. The claim by Plymouth was that some of the return current was leaving the rail and going down into the street causing the sewer and water pipes to be electrolyzed. Apparently this wasn't true because there is no record of any money being paid to Plymouth.

Plant of The Northern Electric Light Co. Norwalk

The interior of the powerhouse in Norwalk of the Cleveland Southwestern and Columbus Railway. (Dennis Lamont)

The SN&M And Receivership

Like most interurban lines in the country, receivership came. Since the SN&M continued to operate at a loss the investors had had enough. On December 12, 1910, a suit was brought against the SN&M by the Title Guarantee and Trust Company of Pittsburgh, in Toledo, Ohio. The road had been in operation 5 years but had made virtually no money. The suit was to foreclose a mortgage in the amount of $600,000. Judge Killets gave the SN&M until December 28 to show why a receiver should not be appointed to oversee the line. As mentioned previously, the Plymouth and Shelby Traction Company, the subsidiary formed to build the line from Plymouth to Shelby, was listed separately only as a defendant along with the Cuyahoga Construction Company that did the construction, and B. B. Avery and Sherman Culp. According to the report filed the average annual deficit of the road was $48,520, an alarming loss. What was also learned is the equipment status. The four Niles combination cars were running but the freight motor was not equipped and had no motor. The mysterious freight motor was mentioned again as the receiver filed for permission to sell the "baggage car". It was sold shortly after. The *Mary Ann* had a snowplow and there were 9 other cars, likely the gondolas used for ballasting the track. The SN&M must have made a convincing argument to the court because no receiver was appointed at this time, and so the SN&M did not officially enter into receivership – yet.

In 1911, the Interstate Commerce Commission ruled that interurbans and railroads could interchange freight. The SN&M saw great potential in this at Norwalk and wished to interchange with the Wheeling and Lake Erie at Benedict Avenue near the powerhouse. On April 14, 1911, they petitioned Norwalk City Council to build an interchange track from Benedict Avenue along the north side of the W&LE to the east where a switch would be installed. Norwalk gave the SN&M a battle which would last a year, in opposition of the interchange track.

Cedar Point Limited Returns

On June 15, 1911 the Cedar Point limited with the Lake Shore Electric returned. This time two cars would run. Each car was a Lake Shore Electric car. Because the orange paint of the LSE cars had faded over the years the newspapers affectionately referred to the limited car as "the big yellow car." The cars rolled north out of Mansfield at 7:30 AM and 1:30 PM. The cars returned to Mansfield at 6:30 PM and 10:30 PM and all of them ran on a two-hour schedule. On July 17, 1911, there was a shake-up with one of these limiteds. While traveling at a fair rate of speed between Shelby and Mansfield the motor suddenly dropped out of the bottom of the car. The car stopped suddenly but nobody was injured. It took a fair amount of time to repair and service was tied up for an entire day. The 1911 edition of the Cedar Point limited did very well according to reports and the last day was Labor Day, September 4, 1911. The Cedar Point limited never ran again.

A rather humorous event occurred in Shelby on July 8, 1911. Apparently president Sherman Culp and the SN&M owed an attorney Jacob Babst of Crestline $1034 since April of that year. Sherman Culp had never paid. Sheriff Sheridan Carroll had been communicating to Culp about this amount due but Culp paid him no mind. Finally on July 8, Carroll had had enough. As the 12:40 PM northbound car out of Shelby, in the charge of motorman James Trimmer and conductor Henry Dildine, pulled past the wye track north of Whitney Avenue, Carroll intercepted them. He had them place the car in the wye track and held the car hostage until that fee was paid. Trimmer and Dildine offered no resistance but rather were quite accommodating putting the car in the wye. After a telegram to Culp was sent, Culp made arrangements to have the money paid. This satisfied Carroll and the car was released.

On August 28, 1911, there was a rather large "smash up" 2 miles south of Norwalk at a location known as Paul's Corners or Stop 28. A work train was on the track at the siding and the motorman thinking it would pull into the siding failed to realize that it was stopped. The passenger car smacked into the back of the work train, shaking up 13 passengers as well as himself. This resulted in a lawsuit.

Sherman Culp Passes Away

Sadly on October 26, 1911, president Sherman Culp of the SN&M passed away in Norwalk at his home having suffered from Bright's Disease. The interurban community was very sad. In honor of Sherman Culp, on October 27, 1911, the SN&M stopped all cars and shut down all substations for a period of 15 minutes from 3:00 PM to 3:15 PM. For 30 days all motormen and conductors wore a black and white rosette on the lapel of their uniforms. The Cleveland Southwestern donated their funeral car, the *Dolores,* to transport Culp's remains from Norwalk to the Plymouth cemetery. Dolores in Spanish means "sorrow" and that is why it was chosen for the name of the funeral car.

Receivership Begins

After the passing of Sherman Culp there was no fighting the operating losses of the SN&M anymore. Employees and bond holders felt somewhat safe with Culp at the helm but those feelings were gone. Judge Killets of Toledo put the SN&M officially into receivership to be handled by receivers C. B. Brooks and Wilbur Hoyt. C. B. Brooks was the treasurer of the SN&M while Wilbur Hoyt was a stock holder; both men resided in North Fairfield. Later a G. B. Dusenberry from Cleveland was added as a third receiver. On April 3, 1912, a Mr. C. G. Taylor was appointed general manager and superintendent of the SN&M by the receivers. C. G. Taylor had previously been the superintendent of the Cleveland Southwestern in Mansfield and Shelby.

Also on April 3, 1912, after a very long battle with Norwalk City Council, the SN&M was granted permission to construct the interchange track with the Wheeling and Lake Erie Railroad on Benedict Avenue. The ordinance stated that the line could turn along Water Street and connect to the Wheeling & Lake Erie. This connection would become very important later. This was the only steam railroad connection ever constructed on the SN&M.

On November 16, 1912, C. G. Taylor was made the sole receiver of the SN&M while Brooks, Hoyt, and Dusenberry resigned. Judge Killets fixed his bond at $5,000. A very important piece to this receivership is the fact that the Plymouth and Shelby Traction Company was not included. It remained entirely separate and at this point. S. S. Burtsfield became president of this subsidiary line, even though technically it was part of the SN&M. It is quite possible this was intentional due to the fact that at receivership the Mansfield Railway, Light & Power Company had become interested in purchasing the P&S line from Shelby to Plymouth. A very odd arrangement was begun on August 16, 1913. The SN&M and M&S began operating "through-cars" from Mansfield to Norwalk. The SN&M provided the cars. The car would operate from Mansfield to Shelby over the M&S and over the P&S to Plymouth and the SN&M for the remaining part into Norwalk. The M&S cars during this odd period only ran from Mansfield to Shelby Junction. There is no doubt that the CSW and MRL&P were testing to see if it was worth purchasing the SN&M. It was not and the "through-service" was discontinued. The next experiment began on October 1, 1913. The "through-service" was cut back to Plymouth with a "through-car" operating from Mansfield to Plymouth connecting to another SN&M car there. This didn't prove profitable either. The whole idea was scrapped on February 16, 1914, and no other "through-service" was ever operated again.

Back in November of 1912, it should be mentioned that the Shelby interurban depot moved from the northwest corner of Main and Mohican to 16 Mohican Street. It was always owned by the M&S line and this was explained in the M&S section.

The 1913 Flood – Structural Damage

On March 24 and 25 of 1913, Ohio experienced one of the worst floods in history. Much of the damage can be read elsewhere and is well-documented but the SN&M suffered severely in the middle of their system. During the rains the west embankment at the bridge over the Huron River gave way. The west abutment of the bridge sank and shifted and thus formed a kink in the track. It was bad enough that cars could not operate over the bridge. Thankfully the SN&M kept at least one car overnight on the Shelby-end of the system and so service could be conducted on both sides of the bridge. However, getting passengers from one car to the other was a problem.

The first solution was very inconvenient. Due to lack of funds it took many weeks for the SN&M to be able to pay for repairs to restore service over the bridge. From the time of the flood well into May of 1913, passengers traveling north to Norwalk from points south had to get off the car at Steuben and walk to a point known as Lovell Station, where the SN&M crossed State Route 61. That was quite a walk and passengers were entirely dissatisfied with that situation. It took until late April-early May of 1913 for the SN&M to be able to provide bussing between Steuben and Lovell Station (and vice versa) and repairs weren't even completed by then. Eventually the line was opened but the abutment could not be fixed completely and the little kink could be noticed. Even to this day, the abutment remains in place and is slanted away from its original position, a reminder of the 1913 flood.

Photo of the Huron River bridge after the water receded (view from the south). (Willard Library)

The SN&M bridge over the Huron River was "kinked" by a shifting bridge abutment on the west end during the flood of 1913. It was never fully repaired. (Willard Library)

Posing on the Huron River bridge east of Steuben looking east, prior to the flood. In the distance the track climbs a steep grade to reach Rt. 61 at grade-level. (Willard Library)

North Fairfield Car Barn Burns

The original North Fairfield car barn and small shops located on the western edge of North Fairfield met its fate on December 26, 1914. At 8:45 AM a blaze began when a tube leading from a gasoline tank to an active blow torch burst. The gasoline quickly caught fire and things were out of control in a hurry. A car being repaired at the time in the car barn was badly damaged but fortunately there were no injuries. The car barn burned to the ground. The SN&M had need to rebuild this facility so various cities lobbied to have it rebuilt in their city such as Norwalk and Chicago Junction. The SN&M decided however to rebuild right there on the old site. Because the SN&M was in receivership this took some time. Finally, on October 30, 1915, the court ordered C. G. Taylor to rebuild the car barn and small repair shop. But it could only be a very small structure and was considered temporary. The smaller structure only cost $1,500 while a new one the size of the old would have been $10,000. It was 70'6" x 24'6" and had a concrete foundation and floor with a car pit. The Beelman Manufacturing and Lumber Company was awarded the contract and construction began shortly after November 4, 1915.

Cars Given Permission to be Rebuilt

On March 29, 1915, Judge Killets ordered the receiver C. G. Taylor to rebuild the "4 remaining cars." Apparently one of the cars, which one isn't known, was rebuilt at the Cleveland Southwestern's Elyria shops. Which car it was and what repairs were done remain a mystery. The repairs on the other three cars are also not known.

Receiver Sale in 1917

Since the receivership had been going on since 1912, the U. S. District Court ordered the line sold by April 15, 1917. There were no takers on this money-losing proposition so the company remained in receivership. The stock holders however purchased the Plymouth and Shelby Traction Company so that the property was officially part of the SN&M, on paper.

Chicago Junction and Willard Explanation of Service

In 1917, the town of Chicago Junction had its name changed by the postmaster to Willard in honor of Baltimore and Ohio president Daniel Willard. (Technically, it was Chicago, Ohio until late 1911, but locals refered to it as Chicago Junction long ago.) Therefore the timetable of the SN&M had been changed and the spur car was now known as the "Willard spur car." It didn't last. Passenger numbers were so low that the SN&M decided to discontinue the dedicated spur car on September 26, 1917. Instead, mainline cars would run into Willard. For example, the northbound car out of Plymouth would pull into Willard from Newman's. After the Willard station stop, the car would back out to Newman's to get back on the mainline. The car would then head north to Norwalk. The reverse was done for southbound cars. Those cars would back into Willard and pull out forward. This was a serious service problem and caused a significant added amount of time to run from Shelby to Norwalk. Ridership was so low, however, it wasn't likely a concern to the SN&M who saw its impending doom.

Also of note is the Willard interurban depot was moved from the Williams Building on the southwest corner of Myrtle and Pearl to 114 Myrtle Avenue which was on the north side of the old Post Office. It was moved again in December of 1919, to 105 Myrtle Avenue which was on the north side of the Willard Times-Junction newspaper building. It would remain there until the end of the SN&M in March of 1921.

SN&M car making a station stop at Chicago Junction at the southwest corner of Myrtle and Pearl. (Willard Library)

For years car #3 was the "spur car" running exclusively from Newman's to Willard, and back. Here is car #3 on Myrtle Avenue posing at Pearl, the location of the original depot. The car is facing south. (Timothy Brian McKee)

The Lake Shore Electric originally had a great relationship with the SN&M and almost tried to control the company. In the early years the LSE loaned equipment to the SN&M. LSE #60, a Brill combine (passenger and freight) was loaned to be used as the Chicago Junction spur car for a time. Here it is posed at Myrtle and Pearl in approximately 1907. (Max Wilcox)

Cars running between Newman's and Chicago Junction/Willard had to either make the inbound trip in reverse or the outbound trip in reverse because there was no wye on the branch at either end. This could cause problems occasionally as shown here. While backing up the flange "clipped" the rail on the curve where the track turned from Myrtle onto Tiffin Avenue in this 1917 scene. (Willard Library)

Same derailment scene as shown in the first photo. Just waiting around for the Mary Ann. (Willard Library)

```
SN&M #3 with two trolley poles as the "Willard Spur Car"
Frank Sharp, Conductor    Scott Mackin, Motorman    Dad Boyle, Agent (far right)
```

Although it didn't solve the running in reverse problem, the SN&M did try to speed things up by adding a second pole to the "spur car." (Dennis Lamont)

Celery was a hot commodity for shipment on the SN&M at Chicago Junction/Willard. (Willard Library)

Newman's was the location where the line to Chicago Junction peeled off the mainline. The switch was located just south of today's Rt. 598/Rt. 103 intersection. In this view north, the spur car is on the left, the southbound car in the middle, and the northbound car on the right. There was no siding here. To perform this meet, the northbound car had to pull into the Chicago Junction spur, let the southbound car by, back out, then continue north. This was an operational headache for years on the SN&M. (Author)

North Fairfield Tragedy

On November 7, 1917, a telephone line repairman by the name of William Bauman was working in North Fairfield next to the substation. While working with some telephone lines he accidentally crossed one of them with the high tension line over the SN&M poles and was severely electrocuted. He perished instantly. He was only 26 years old and had a wife and two children. It was said that the big Elyria powerplant on the CSW had to be shut down (which fed the Norwalk plant) in order to remove his body from the wires.

The next year, on May 28, 1918, saw another tragedy for the SN&M occur near North Fairfield. The Watts family was traveling in an automobile driven by the father, Orion Watts, with wife Sarah and sons Vaughn and Lane at approximately 10:30 PM. They were driving on Hanville Corners Road and as they approached Hanville Corners, where that road crosses New State Road and the interurban, an SN&M car was speeding northbound out of North Fairfield. Orion attempted to cross in front of the interurban car but the car stalled on the track. The SN&M crew consisted of Sam Noble, motorman, and Louis White, conductor. The motors were thrown in reverse but it was too late and the interurban struck the automobile with a terrible impact. It was said that the entire family perished.

North Fairfield mill and elevator located on the southwest corner of the square. The SN&M track is elevated on piers on the right. (Dennis Lamont)

And if that wasn't enough, during the summer of 1918, a mail carrier by the name of William Boice out of Chicago Junction, was struck and killed by an SN&M car two miles south of Steuben. The crew were motorman Scott Mackin and conductor Ray Parrett.

North Fairfield Mill and Elevator

The Farmers Elevator was constructed in North Fairfield in 1919, on the southwest corner of the square. This was a grain and feed elevator to serve the North Fairfield area farmers. The elevator used coal for heat and power. This was an excellent opportunity for the SN&M to do freight service. A siding was constructed into the elevator property. The end of the siding was elevated so that coal could be dumped. The SN&M would get carloads of coal from the Wheeling and Lake Erie Railroad at the Norwalk interchange and haul the cars to the elevator where they were unloaded. Grain could also be loaded here and taken back to the W&LE in Norwalk to be shipped. The SN&M always used their own gondola cars for this service. Unfortunately the SN&M wasn't fast enough so the elevator closed just four years later, in 1923, and was moved south to Boughtonville on the B&O.

The work motor Mary Ann was vital to the success of the freight business of the SN&M. Shown here is a work train along Norwalk Road (New State Road) just south of Norwalk. The cars are being hauled from the Wheeling and Lake Erie interchange in Norwalk to the mill in North Fairfield. (Dennis Lamont)

On Into Abandonment

Ridership on the SN&M had dropped off so severely there was really no purpose left for the poor interurban line. Several things were happening in 1920. A foreclosure hearing was set and C. G. Taylor had no defense this time. The court ordered the road junked and appraised for scrap value. The Cleveland Southwestern was supplying the SN&M with power but the SN&M was unable to pay their bills. However, the SN&M continued to sell that electricity for profit themselves. The CSW was not very happy with this. They notified the SN&M that power would be shut off at midnight on March 26, 1921. Knowing full well that they'd never be able to pay a power bill it was announced on March 23, 1921, that the last day of operations would be March 25. C. G. Taylor had gained approval by Judge Killets to junk the line on March 24, but the junking had to be done methodically. The last car did run March 25, 1921, in the charge of motorman James Trimmer. James Trimmer would transfer to the Lake Shore Electric and would make its last run on May 15, 1938. The abandonment crippled the North Fairfield elevator without the freight cars and the SN&M selling electricity to North Fairfield; the residents were now in the dark.

Bus Replacement

The story of the SN&M is not over, however. Although the SN&M itself was gone there would be a small revival in the line later, as will be explained. In the meantime, in April of 1921, the SN&M was directly replaced by a bus service. A bus left Shelby every morning for Norwalk at 8:30 AM and 2 hours thereafter until 8:30 PM. This was known as the Rapid Transit Bus Line. Another bus line began operations from Willard to Plymouth and back and was known as the Independent Bus Line.

Cars Survive

Mystery still surrounds car #5. Its early history is not well-understood but it is known that it ended up on the Ohio Public Service's roster as car #50 on their Toledo, Port Clinton, and Lakeside Railway line (OPS took control in 1924). Car #5 was thought to be the "freight motor" on the line and it appears to have been sold to the Toledo, Port Clinton, and Lakeside prior to OPS ownership, perhaps as early as 1911-1912. The complicating factor is that the original Toledo, Port Clinton, and Lakeside Railway was sold in 1912 and became the Northwestern Ohio Railway and Power Company. The Ohio Public Service purchased this line in September of 1924. At any rate, #50 on the OPS was used as the line car for overhead repairs. After the SN&M was abandoned, the OPS on the same line purchased SN&M car #4 in 1924. It is not known where it was during the 2-3 years prior to being sold after the discontinuance of the SN&M. This was numbered OPS #90 and served as the wreck car. Later the OPS abandoned the TPC&L line from Clay Center to Marblehead, and the line remaining from Toledo to the big limestone quarry in Clay Center was reorganized and named the Toledo and Eastern. These cars were rebuilt into smaller freight motors. They each retained their numbers from OPS but were scrapped in 1958, when the line folded. All the other SN&M equipment appears to have been scrapped upon abandonment.

Disposition of Power

As was mentioned the village of North Fairfield was purchasing electricity from the SN&M. This was done through a separate 10-horsepower motor in the North Fairfield substation. After the power was shut off by the CSW at abandonment North Fairfield was left in the dark. A group of North Fairfield citizens formed the North Fairfield Light Company and purchased some of the power equipment. The group bought the substation and equipment as well as the high tension line from Norwalk to a point about one mile south of Steuben and began selling power again. Long story short is this eventually ended up being purchased by Ohio Edison. The men who formed the company were C. R. Irwin, Dr. L. L. Jones, Charley Harvey, Jack Lafferty, and William J. Wilkinson.

Motormen From 1905 – 1921

The motormen were: James Trimmer, Drew Mickel, Scott Mackin, Wesly Ritter, Frank Wade, Lawrence Morfot, Wade Boyd, Hirman Williams, John Smith, Delbert Burdge, Roy Morrow, Alex Mitchell, Harry Clutter, Cliff Oates, Louis White, Warren Romig, Charley Jones, Howard Snively.

Conductors From 1905 – 1921

The conductors were: Albert Thomas, Charles Stower, R. J. Parratt, George Travis, Clyde Morrow, Chauncey Hamilton, Frank Sharp, Clarence Seidel, Harry Dawson, Will Heston, Raymond McCammon, Ray Jennings, Lester Wright, Henry Dildine, George Dehr, Louis White, Lee Jennings, Wayne Earl, Ed Hinckley, Harry Underwood, Orlie Underwood, Harley Barre, and Albert Shadel.

North Fairfield Substation – Equipment at Abandonment From Final Inventory

One 300 kW, 3-phase, 600 Volt, 500 Amp type S. C. 6-rotary converter with Bullock #18331 resistance coils.

Three 110 kW oil-cooled 3-phase transformers.

One G. E. 2 ½ kV A-transformer (220-100 V).

One single-phase 110 V, 7 ½ kW generator with 1-2 kW exciter for above generator.

Plymouth Substation – Equipment at Abandonment From Final Inventory

One 300 kW, 3-phase, 300 Volt, 500 Amp type S. C. 6-rotary converter with Bullock #18331 resistance coils.

Three 110 kW oil-cooled transformers.

Building – 20' x 20' frame with tarred paper and gravel roof, cement foundations.

More Photos

A southbound SN&M car comes down the hill into North Fairfield. It will cross the bridge over a small stream and then enter North Main Street at the village corporation limits. (Dennis Lamont)

Northbound SN&M car on North Main Street in North Fairfield in the 1909 "mini-blizzard." (Willis McCaleb)

Northbound car on North Main Street in North Fairfield in approximately 1909. That's another Hoyt's residence to the left in the photo, a well-known local family name. (Author)

Westbound SN&M car #4 on West Main Street in North Fairfield. (Dennis Lamont)

Eastbound car coming into North Fairfield on West Main Street. The gentleman appears to be excited to have his picture taken. (Dennis Lamont)

A southbound car on the B&O overpass at Newman's. This view is looking north and that is Peru Center Road crossing the B&O next to the bridge. (Willard Library)

This photo is looking west down the B&O with an overhead northbound SN&M car at Newman's. The farmer is southbound on Peru Center Road. (Willard Library)

This dramatic view shows a southbound SN&M car pulling into the New Haven depot, located in the first building on the left. We're looking north up Rt. 61 from the Rt. 224 intersection in 1909. (Author)

Southbound SN&M car #1 at New Haven. The car is stopped in front of the freight shed while the passenger depot is on the right out of sight. (Shelby Museum of History)

Motorman Scott Mackin and Conductor Lee Jennings pose with car #3 in Chicago Junction at Myrtle and Pearl. Note that at this time #3 has two poles. (Dennis Lamont)

In Chicago Junction in 1912, an SN&M car follows a Decoration Day parade up Myrtle Avenue. (Author)

Southbound SN&M car on Sandusky Street in Plymouth. (Plymouth Area Historical Society)

Northbound SN&M car on the square in Plymouth, passing the bandstand. (Timothy Brian McKee)

Northbound car from Shelby coming into Plymouth in the teens. A very nice artistic angle. (Plymouth Area Historical Society)

Northbound SN&M heads away from the photographer, crossing the Northern Ohio Railroad (later the AC&Y and W&LE). This dramatic photo was taken by Max Wilcox. (Author)

Shelby Spring Hinge & Brightman Factory, Shelby, Ohio

View west on East Smiley Street in Shelby in 1909. The SN&M crosses the B&O and then swerves over to join the Mansfield-Shelby interurban. The Springe Hinge Company is on the left and the Brightman Manufacturing is on the right. (Shelby Museum of History)

The only known photo of an SN&M car in Shelby is shown here. The car is westbound on East Smiley running along the remains of the Brightman Manufacturing Company which burned in 1910. (Shelby Museum of History)

SN&M "gold bond" preferred stock. Imagine these ever being worth $100.

Sandusky, Norwalk & Mansfield Electric Railway Time Card.

NORTH-BOUND. (In effect July 18, 1908)

	a.m.	a.m.	Lim't'd. a.m.	a.m.	a.m.	a.m.	p.m.	p.m.	p.m.	p.m.	p.m.	p.m.	p.m.	p.m.
Mansfield			7:30											
Shelby	5:30	6:50	8:00	8:20	9:50	11:20	12:50	2:20	3:50	5:20	6:50	8:20	9:50	11:35
Plymouth	5:50	7:15	8:18	8:45	10:15	11:45	1:15	2:45	4:15	5:45	7:15	8:45	10:15	11:55
New Haven	5:55	7:20	8:21	8:50	10:20	11:50	1:20	2:50	4:20	5:50	7:20	8:50	10:20	12:00
Newman's	6:00	7:25	8:25	8:55	10:25	11:55	1:25	2:55	4:25	5:55	7:25	8:55	10:25	12:05
Steuben	6:07	7:32		9:02	10:32	12:02	1:32	3:02	4:32	6:02	7:32	9:02	10:32	12:12
N. Fairfield	6:15	7:40	8:37	9:10	10:40	12:10	1:40	3:10	4:40	6:10	7:40	9:10	10:40	12:20
Norwalk	6:35	8:00	9:00	9:30	11:00	12:30	2:00	3:30	5:00	6:30	8:00	9:30	11:00	
Sandusky			9:50											
Ar. Chicago Jct.	6:10	7:35	8:35	9:05	10:35	12:05	1:35	3:05	4:35	6:05	7:35	9:05	10:35	12:15
Lv. Chicago Jct.	5:35	7:15	8:10	8:45	10:15	11:45	1:15	2:45	4:15	5:45	7:15	8:45	10:15	11:50

SOUTH-BOUND (In effect July 18, 1908)

	a.m.	a.m.	a.m.	a.m.	a.m.	p.m.	p.m.	Lim't'd p.m.	p.m.	p.m.	p.m.	p.m.	p.m.
Sandusky								6:45					
Norwalk		6:45	8:15	9:45	11:15	12:45	2:15	7:35	3:45	5:15	6:45	8:15	9:45	11:25
N. Fairfield	5:30	7:07	8:37	10:07	11:37	1:07	2:37	7:53	4:07	5:37	7:07	8:37	10:07	11:45
Steuben	5:37	7:15	8:45	10:15	11:45	1:15	2:45		4:15	5:45	7:15	8:45	10:15	11:55
Newman's	5:50	7:25	8:55	10:25	11:55	1:25	2:55	8:10	4:25	5:55	7:25	8:55	10:25	12:05
New Haven	5:53	7:28	8:58	10:28	11:58	1:28	2:58	8:12	4:28	5:58	7:28	8:58	10:28	12:08
Plymouth	6:00	7:35	9:05	10:35	12:05	1:35	3:05	8:17	4:35	6:05	7:35	9:05	10:35	12:15
Shelby	6:25	8:00	9:30	11:00	12:30	2:00	3:30	8:35	5:00	6:30	8:00	9:30	11:00	12:30
Mansfield								9:05						

CONNECTIONS.

SHELBY—Electric. Mansfield & Shelby Electric Ry. Every hour.
NORWALK—Electric. Lake Shore and Cleveland & Southwestern. Every hour.
PLYMOUTH—B. & O. West; 8:45 a. m., 10:48 a. m., 4:33 p. m., 10:43 p. m.
 " B. & O. East; 4:10 a. m., 9:23 a. m., 4:51 p. m., 9:00 p. m.
 " Northern Ohio Ry., West; 7:00 a. m., 11:55 a. m.
 " " East; 6:00 p. m., 1:10 p. m.
SHELBY—Big Four, East; a. m.—12:06 4:37 6:59 9:25 10:42. p. m.—1:47 7:36 8:36
 " " West; a. m.—4:25 8:23. p. m.—2:08 5:59 6:26 7:32 10:53

July 18, 1908 schedule issued with connections listed at the bottom. Service was frequent.

102

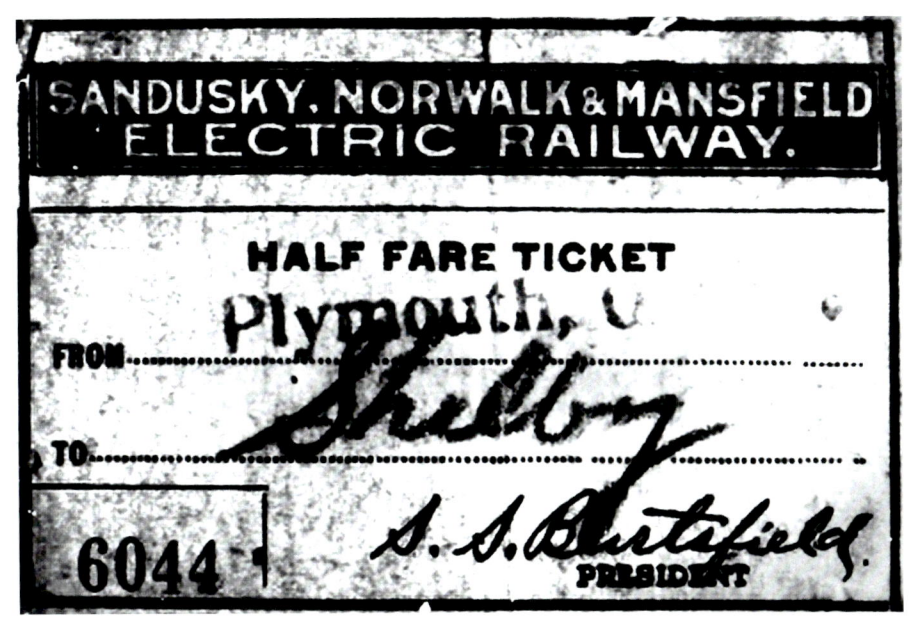

Special "half fare" ticket good from Plymouth to Shelby. (Dennis Lamont)

The SN&M did what were called fare receipts. The passenger purchased a ticket and boarded the car. When the passenger got off the car at his or her stop, the conductor punched the number next to the stop. There were many stops so the receipt was divided into sections; each section contained a number of stops. The receipt was perforated down the middle and at the stop, the passenger kept the left-hand side and the conductor the right.

PART III
THE NORWALK AND SHELBY RAILROAD COMPANY

With the SN&M gone and the expectation that no more cars would ever operate over the route, the Big Four Railroad pulled up the crossing in Shelby. The SN&M had still owed the Big Four approximately $428 for a crossing improvement. All the rails were left in elsewhere, but the poles and overhead equipment as well as the power equipment were slowly dismantled.

The SN&M property was auctioned off on October 29, 1921, at Plymouth. Henry Weir of Sandusky and I. Wilkoff of Canton purchased the entire property for $60,500. What they had planned for the line at the time was unknown. The town of Willard wanted some answers as to what these gentlemen were doing with the rails because they needed to improve their subway under the B&O on Tiffin Street. On May 18, 1922, still no word from the two gentlemen was heard.

On June 22, 1922, the full plans were announced. A new company called The Norwalk and Shelby Railroad Company was incorporated by C. R. Irwin of North Fairfield along with capitalists J. L. Baugh and Company of Indianapolis. It was also announced at this time that the company would not operate interurban cars by electric but rather by gasoline-powered interurban coaches. According to Baugh, operating these would cost 1/3 that of an electric interurban car. Bonds were issued on July 9, 1922, and most of them were purchased by Plymouth and Plymouth area residents. In August of 1922, crews began cleaning up the right-of-way and repairing track for upcoming use. On September 5, 1922, the official meeting of the Norwalk and Shelby Railroad was held in North Fairfield. The following officers were named: J. L. Baugh, president; C. E. Heath, vice president; A. D. Sanders, secretary; C. R. Irwin, treasurer; A. B. Bowen, R. L. Castor, W. B. Keefer, and A. J. Ellery on the board of directors. Several manufacturers of these gasoline cars were examined. The American Railway Car Company of Elyria was ultimately chosen. At first the company ordered three cars but that order was cut back to two. The first car from American arrived in Norwalk on October 31, 1922. The car was 35 feet long and weighed 28,000 lbs. The coach area could hold 40 people and it had a gasoline engine capable of 35 mph. The second car didn't arrive until December 22, 1922, on opening day. The cars were numbered 1 and 2.

The Willard mayor was very excited about the coming of the Norwalk and Shelby Railroad. He had a parade and gave a speech in late November. The depot was moved to the Hoffman Hotel at the intersection of Myrtle and Maple and sat on the southwest corner. The building remains today.

Opening day finally came on December 22, 1922. The issue with the NYC Big Four in Shelby however, hadn't been resolved. The N&S had to pay to put in the crossing which took more time. A problem that would not go away either was the fact that the old SN&M owed the NYC Big Four $428.21 for a prior crossing improvement, as mentioned. Knowing that the crossing could not be installed by opening day, a wye track was constructed along State Street in Shelby just north of the Big Four so that cars could turn. A taxi met the gasoline cars there and took the passengers into Shelby. Likewise, passengers were taken out to State Street where the gasoline cars would be boarded. Many were excited according to the newspapers. It was touted that the gasoline cars could run on that snowy and icy day, while interurbans could not because ice had accumulated on the overhead wires of many other lines.

Manufacturer's photo of Norwalk & Shelby Railroad Company car #1. (Shelby Museum of History)

Manufacturer's photo of Norwalk & Shelby Railroad Company car #1. (Shelby Museum of History)

Opening day for the Norwalk & Shelby Railroad Company at the North Fairfield depot on December 22, 1922. (Shelby Museum of History)

Shelby had two opening days due to the Big Four crossing trouble. On December 22, 1922, cars could only operate to State Street, where a temporary wye was constructed to turn the cars. Here, passengers boarded a taxi to the interurban depot on Mohican Street. The crew poses at the wye. (Author)

Meanwhile, on January 18, 1923, interurban depot agent Albert Gray in Shelby was appointed to assistant general manager of the N&S despite already being an employee of the Ohio Public Service at Shelby.

On January 20, 1923, the crossing was finally put in over the NYC Big Four tracks in Shelby. The gasoline cars could now operate all the way to the Mohican Street depot in Shelby. This was a "second opening day" of sorts because it was the first time the gasoline car motored down Mohican Street to the depot. The wye track was removed at State Street. At this point it was decided to have the cars refuel at the Shelby interurban depot. R. E. Marquis, head of Standard Oil in Shelby, connected the hoses to a pump to be used there.

Shelby's second opening day was January 21, 1923. The Big Four crossing had been reinstalled the previous evening and now the gasoline cars could operate to the interurban depot on Mohican Street. Pictured here are (left to right) motorman Cecil Freese, conductor Raymond McCammon, and station agent Albert Gray. The switch in the background is the wye on Mohican Street located just north of Whitney Avenue. (Shelby Museum of History)

On May 31, 1923, an odd announcement was made. The N&S decided to haul a freight trailer and needed a third gasoline car. They approached the Fate-Root-Heath Company of Plymouth (later Plymouth locomotive) about manufacturing a car. The car unfortunately was never built and freight service never began.

It is known that a third car was eventually ordered and arrived in Norwalk and was delivered to Willard on September 15, 1923, for service from Willard out to Newman's like in the old SN&M days. Not much is known about the spur car as it was called but it did suffer mechanical trouble quite often. In fact so did the other two cars. Throughout the life of the N&S, cars were taken in and out of service many, many times due to mechanical problems.

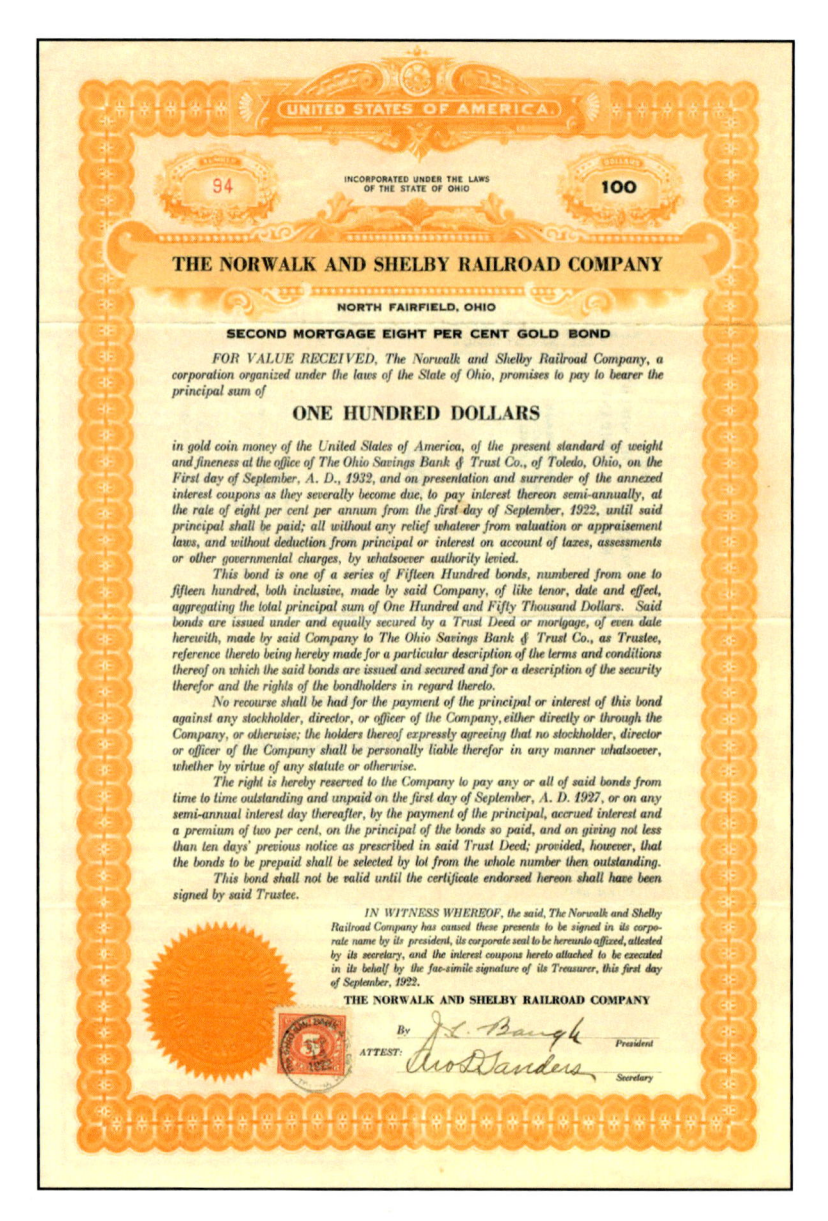

Just like the SN&M, the Norwalk and Shelby Railroad was performing very poorly. As has been stated many times before, the automobile competition was too much for the weak little gasoline line. Due to operating losses and the failure of the ability to pay the Big Four at Shelby the $428.21, the N&S was thrown into receivership. On November 4, 1923, Huron County Common Pleas Judge Irving Carpenter appointed Edgar G. Martin receiver of the road. E. G. Martin was an attorney in Norwalk. Operations would continue as normal for the time being.

On February 4, 1924, Judge Irving Carpenter then ordered a foreclosure and the property to be put up for sale. The Wilkoff Syndicate of Youngstown was the holder of the mortgages on the property. The equipment listed at this time were the two main gasoline coaches and the little Willard spur car. But on February 21, 1924, the spur car was discontinued and replaced by Emmett L. Guthrie's taxi line.

Abandonment Looms

On March 1, 1924, E. G. Martin, receiver, filed a motion with the Public Utilities Commission of Ohio to abandon the gasoline line. The commission later granted permission and a foreclosure sale was set to take place at the Huron County Courthouse on April 17, 1924. The last gasoline cars did run on April 17 and that was the last day. The Morrison-Risman Company of Buffalo purchased the entire property for $53,800. The company had no intention of operating the line and everything was scrapped. Rail removal began on August 3, 1924, in Plymouth, by the Weirs Scrap Metal Company of Sandusky.

Riding the Sandusky, Norwalk, and Mansfield Electric Railway Today

If one wishes to follow this long-forgotten interurban line there are still outstanding relics. Cars always began from the south end at the Shelby interurban depot. Cars rolled north on Mohican Street and passed the wye location described in the M&S section. Turning east onto East Smiley the switch was passed where the M&S line turned north and went to the NYC Big Four depot. SN&M cars continued east and clicked across the Baltimore and Ohio Railroad diamonds running up to Second Street. At Second Street the line turns north, still in the middle of the pavement. Second Street dead ends at Elm but the SN&M continued north across the NYC Big Four (now CSX) and State Street. The right-of-way is very visible at State Street and this is where the temporary wye was installed at the beginning of the Norwalk and Shelby Railroad. From here the route continues north on Second Street Extension but where that street ends the SN&M arched to the northwest across a yard to join the east side of Broadway at Cline. The line stays on the east side of Broadway and crosses London West Road and then across the western part of the reservoir heading for Route 61. The SN&M crossed the Black Fork behind the reservoir and there is a cut in the woods and powerlines on the right-of-way. Difficult to locate, concrete ruins are buried where there was a bridge across the stream. The line then heads up an access road and crosses Bistline Road, then immediately joins the east side of Route 61. Just beyond Hazelbrush Road the line swerves over to the west side of Route 61. The best relic is beyond Henry Road. Between Henry and Opdyke, a large ravine is encountered. Rather than build a fill and bridge across the ravine, the interurban line "bows" westward and arcs around the ravine to rejoin Route 61 on the southwest corner of 61 and Opdyke Road. Bridge abutments still stand at Opdyke at the stream. The roadbed on the arc here is well cleared, and with permission, this private right-of-way can be walked. The lake along the bow was the site of the Huron Valley Park and the grade going north across Opdyke Road was known as Kirkpatrick's Hill.

The SN&M remains on the west side of the road to the Plymouth corporation limits. The southern limits are unchanged since interurban days and this is where the SN&M went to the middle of the street, running into the Plymouth square. On the west side of the street, two lots north of the square, was the Smith Hotel. The first floor was used as the interurban depot, ticket office, and waiting room. The agents were Mr. Smith of the Smith Hotel and Burt Shadel. The interurban also did a fantastic Wells Fargo Express service here. This was also the original 1905 southern terminal of the line prior to the Shelby extension. Proceeding north out of Plymouth the tracks left the street exactly where the sidewalk ends today across from Community Markets. This is also where the Plymouth siding was located; it was involved in the wreck on August 28, 1908, explained elsewhere.

The interurban remained on the west side of Route 61 again but only to a point just south of the New Haven cemetery. Just before reaching Skinner Road the powerlines today cross over to the east side of Route 61 and that's where the interurban ran. The SN&M is now on the east side of Route 61 to New Haven.

The depot at New Haven was located in a store front affair on the west side of Rt. 61 just north of

Prairie Street and slightly opposite the Odd Fellow's Hall. The depot remains in part today as a home. A freight shed was located across the street from the depot and one lot north of the Odd Fellow's Hall since the track was on the opposite side of the road of the passenger depot. The agents over the years were Fred Dawson and James Palmer. Continuing north out of New Haven the SN&M remains on the east side of the road, now Rt. 598. A steel bridge was constructed over Marsh Run but nothing remains. Approaching Route 103 a big brick house stands on the right. This is where the "switch" began for the Chicago Junction or Willard spur. The location was known as Newman's in interurban days. Here, a passenger could transfer to the spur car to go to Chicago Junction or stay on the current car and continue to Norwalk.

Running west to Willard the line joined the south side of Route 103 at a point just west of the Rt. 598/Rt. 103 intersection. It followed the south side of 103 all the way to the corporation line, where it entered the street. This is also where 103 became Tiffin Avenue. However, back at the B&O (now Ashland Railway) underpass look closely at the south side. The interurban had its own passage under the B&O, not common with the road, and the outline can be seen today.

Proceeding into Willard the line simply turned north on Myrtle Avenue, now in the center of the street. The original line ended at the intersection of Myrtle and Pearl. For years the depot was on the southwest corner known as the Williams Building which is now a parking lot. On December 27, 1906 the track was extended north beyond this point to a point 3 buildings north of Maple Avenue. However, the ticket office and waiting room remained at Pearl in the Williams Building. The depot wasn't moved until November 1917, when it went to 114 Myrtle Avenue. It moved again in December of 1919 to 105 Myrtle Avenue. And finally after the Norwalk and Shelby Railroad gasoline line began, it was moved another time to Hoffman's Hall on the southwest corner of Myrtle and Maple. The agents from 1905 to 1924 were Mr. Evans and Dad Boyle.

Going back out to the mainline at Newman's this time we will finish the trip to Norwalk. Continuing north from Rt. 103 the line clearly rises up onto a large fill for the overpass that was built over the B&O Railroad in 1906. This was also the location of the Newman saga. After the line comes back down to road level it follows the east side of Peru Center Road to Maple Ridge Road. Here, the line crossed Maple Ridge and then immediately swerves to the west side of Peru Center Road. This was the location of the Maple Ridge depot/shelter built in 1905. The line, now on the west side of Peru Center, continues to Steuben. Approaching the main intersection the line suddenly crosses the road and heads diagonally northeast along the fence row and across Rt. 162. On the north side of Rt. 162 was the depot for the SN&M along with a siding. The Steuben agent was a Mr. Searles. The home here on the right-of-way faces west and this is because this was Steuben's second SN&M depot after the original was replaced. It still stands today. It is not known when or why the first depot was replaced. The line then runs behind the former school and aims straight east picking up the old Clinton Air Line Railroad grade just slightly northeast of the old school building. It runs east through the Steuben "cut" where there are bridge abutments over a small stream. The SN&M now on the Clinton Air Line is a few hundred feet north of Rt. 162 but in parallel.

The line continues east across the Huron River. This was a rather large steel bridge and there are outstanding relics if one wishes to hike to this point. There were two concrete abutments on each side of the river and two piers flanking the river. Two of the piers and the west abutment remain. Ahead the line approaches Route 61 and at this point the SN&M climbs out of the Huron River valley and leaves the Clinton Air Line Railroad. The SN&M curves sharply to the southeast at Route 61, crosses Route 162, and then joins the south side of 162 for the trek into North Fairfield. A big fill had to be built approaching Ridge Road due to the terrain. Just past Ridge Road the Clinton Air Line RR right-of-way is crossed, although at this point nothing remains of that railroad. Ahead at the western village limits of North Fairfield, on the right will be the remains of the second, "temporary" car barn that replaced the original that burned in 1914. The red barn as of this date can be seen on the south side of the road. Here the SN&M went into the middle of the street.

Running into North Fairfield the line went to the square and then turned diagonally along the edge of the northwest corner and then went north in the middle of New State Road. On the northwest corner was the large, ornate passenger depot, ticket office, waiting room, and dispatcher's office. Behind that structure was the substation. On the southwest corner was the location of the North Fairfield mill and elevator. The interurban began serving the elevator portion in 1919, as described elsewhere. The agents here were Cliff Oates from 1905 to 1907, William J. Wilkinson from 1905 to 1919, and J. Alto Rogers from 1907 to 1921.

Heading north on New State Road (North Main) was a siding located just north of the square to stage gondolas and dump cars for the gravel pit, or the W&LE RR interchange in Norwalk. The SN&M swerved to the west side of the road just before reaching the stream. Immediately after leaving the street the interurban went over the stream on its own bridge, and both concrete abutments remain today. The stretch along New State Road is one of the most fascinating sections on the SN&M as numerous concrete bridge abutments remain. Unfortunately just south of Hanville Corners there is no evidence of the gravel pit as that land has all been filled.

The SN&M stayed faithfully on the west side of New State to Ridge Road where it then took the west side of Ridge north toward Norwalk. Past South Norwalk Road and before the US 20 bypass overpass, on the west side of the road is a large concrete arch bridge over the stream and valley, remaining as it was in interurban days (built to last).

The line simply ran into Norwalk along the street. After the US 20 overpass, the street becomes Norwood Avenue. At the city limits is where the interurban went to the center of the street. The line turned north on Benedict at that intersection. As mentioned in 1912, a connection track was built with the W&LE on the north side of the railroad. The Cleveland Southwestern powerhouse was on the south side of the railroad a few hundred feet east of the Benedict Avenue crossing. After crossing the W&LE Railroad, on the left is 46 Benedict Avenue where the SN&M depot was moved in 1909. Since there was never a wye track at this location, cars had to run up to Main Street to turn the cars at Benedict and Main on the LSE-owned wye track there. Prior to 1909, the LSE and SN&M shared depots at 12 East Main Street, one lot just east of the present courthouse. The dedicated SN&M agents are not known, but the SN&M bookkeepers in Norwalk were Hazel Burdge and Alma Bush.

KEY MAPS OF THE SN&M FROM SHELBY TO NORWALK

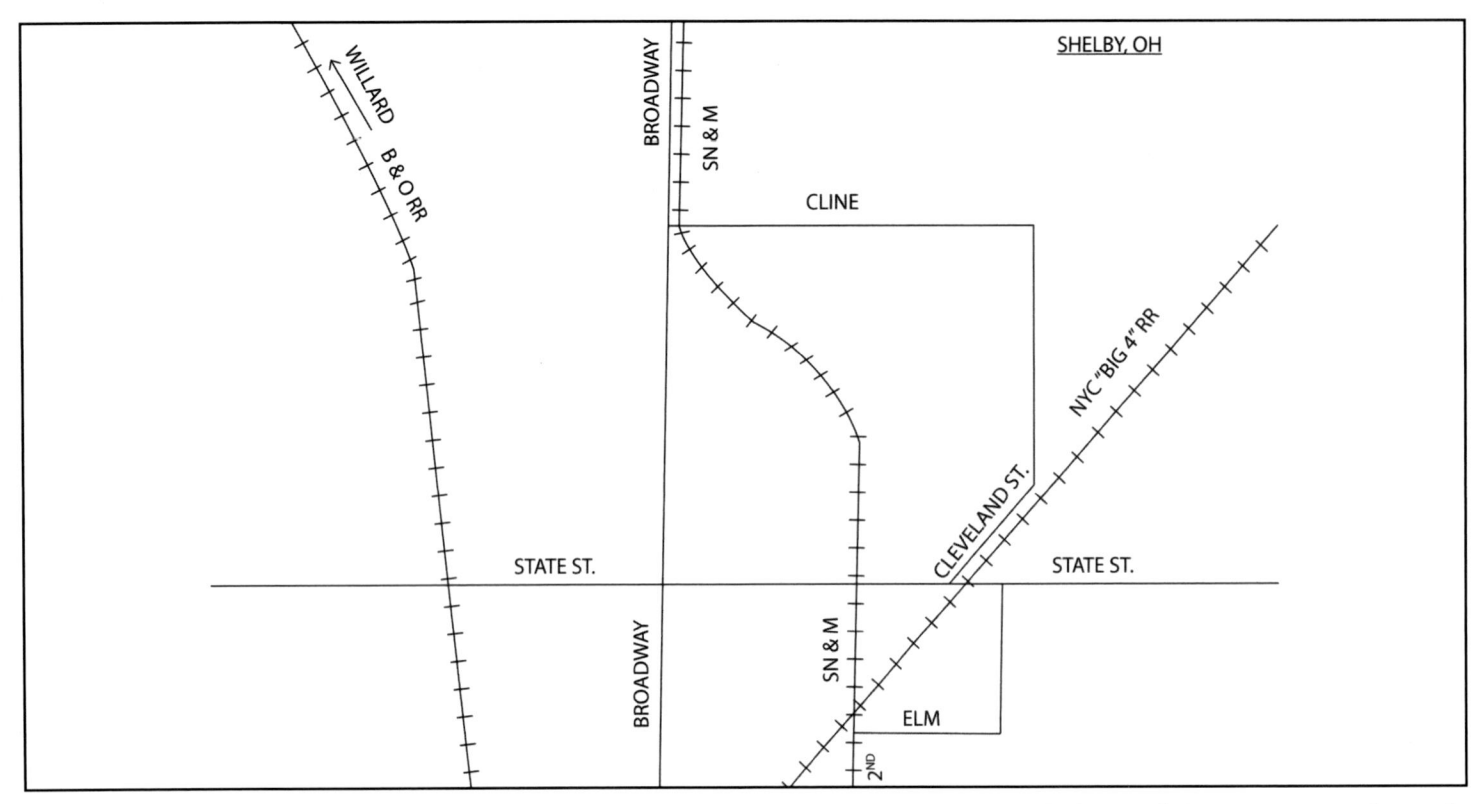

After the SN&M ran north on Second Street in Shelby, it crossed the Big 4 and then State Street. The line angled over to join North Broadway at Cline.

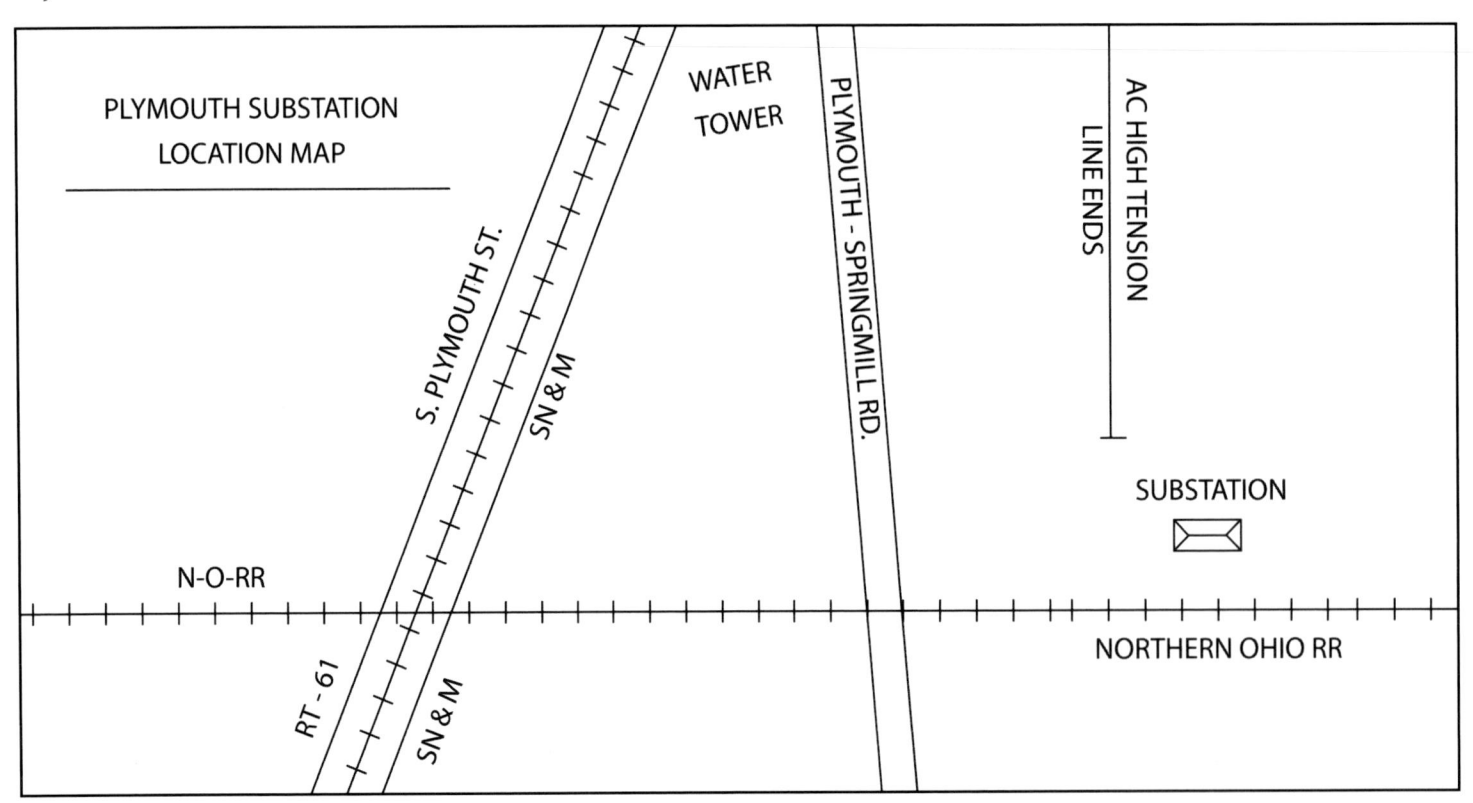

At Plymouth, the substation was east of the SN&M by an unusual distance. It was located on the north side of the railroad east of Plymouth-Springmill Road. Plymouth prohibited the SN&M's high-tension powerlines from coming through the main part of the village necessitating the substation to be east of the main right-of-way. The AC line originally ended here.

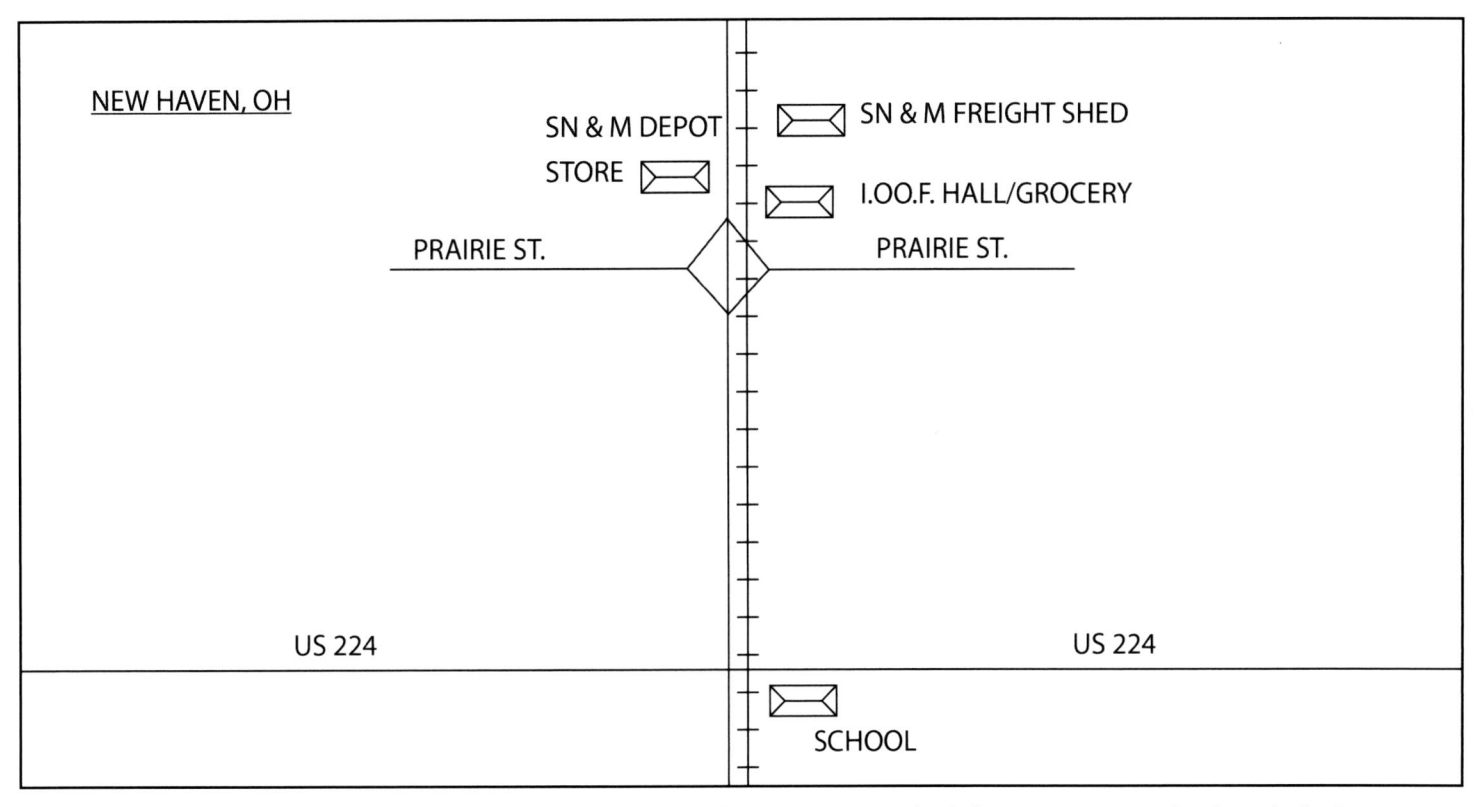

New Haven was simple. After the SN&M crossed to the east side of Route 61 just south of Skinner, it ran straight along the highway through the village. The depot was opposite the Odd Fellow's Hall in a store. The freight shed was just north of the Odd Fellow's Hall.

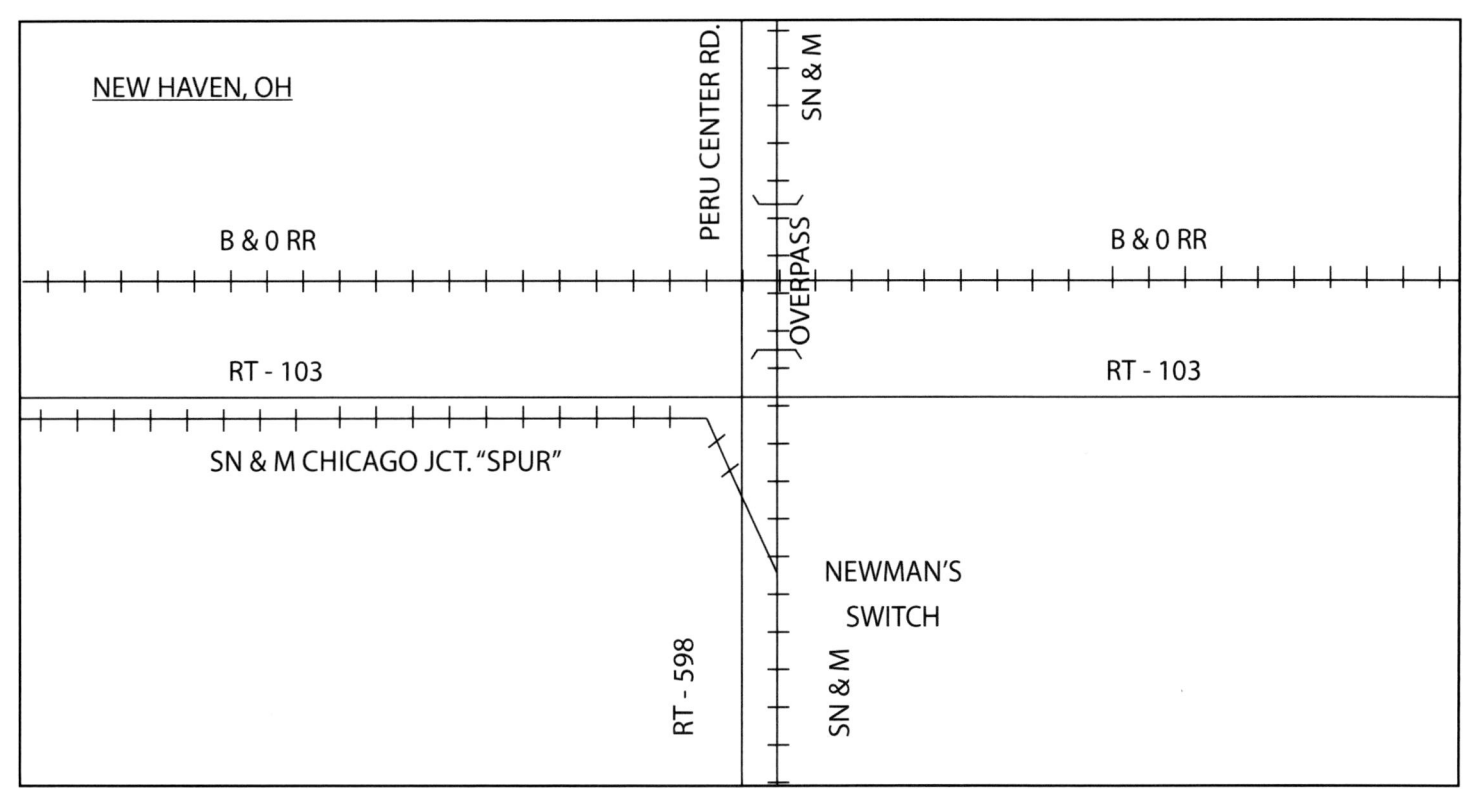

Newman was at the intersection of Rt. 598 and Rt. 103. This is where the "spur" track to Chicago Junction/Willard peeled westward. Going north the SN&M went over the B&O on a steel bridge.

CHICAGO JUNCTION, OH
WILLARD, OH

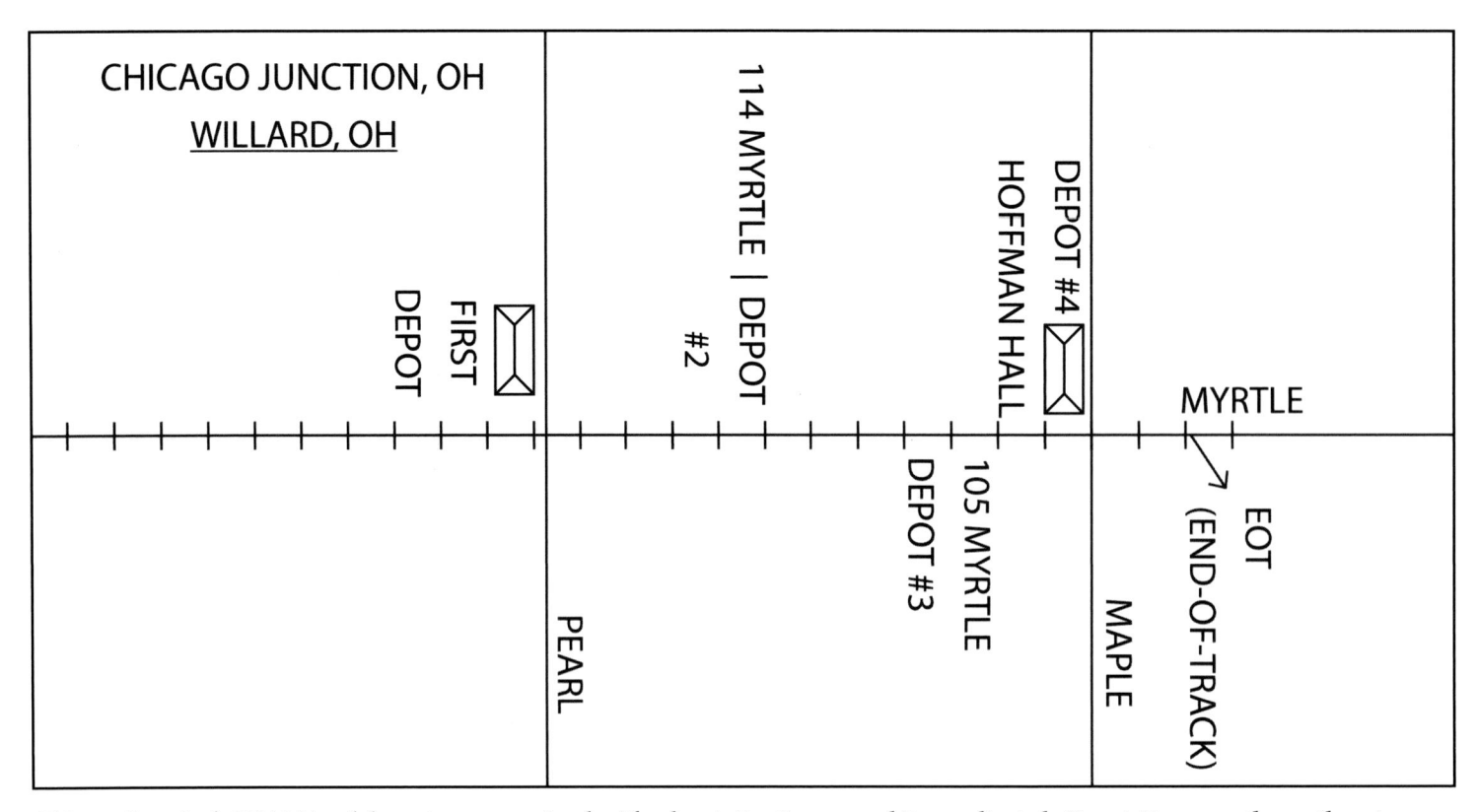

[Map showing Myrtle Avenue with: FIRST DEPOT, 114 MYRTLE / DEPOT #2, PEARL, 105 MYRTLE / DEPOT #3, HOFFMAN HALL / DEPOT #4, MAPLE, EOT (END-OF-TRACK)]

Chicago Junction's SN&M track layout was very simple. The depot situation was a bit complicated. Depot #1 was on the southwest corner of Myrtle and Pearl in a building called the Williams building from 1905 to 1917. It was then moved to 114 Myrtle Avenue (#2). In 1919, it again moved to #3 at 105 Myrtle Avenue. After the Norwalk & Shelby Railroad was formed the depot was housed in the Hoffman Hotel at location #4 on the southwest corner of Myrtle and Maple. The track stub-ended just north of Maple as indicated in the map.

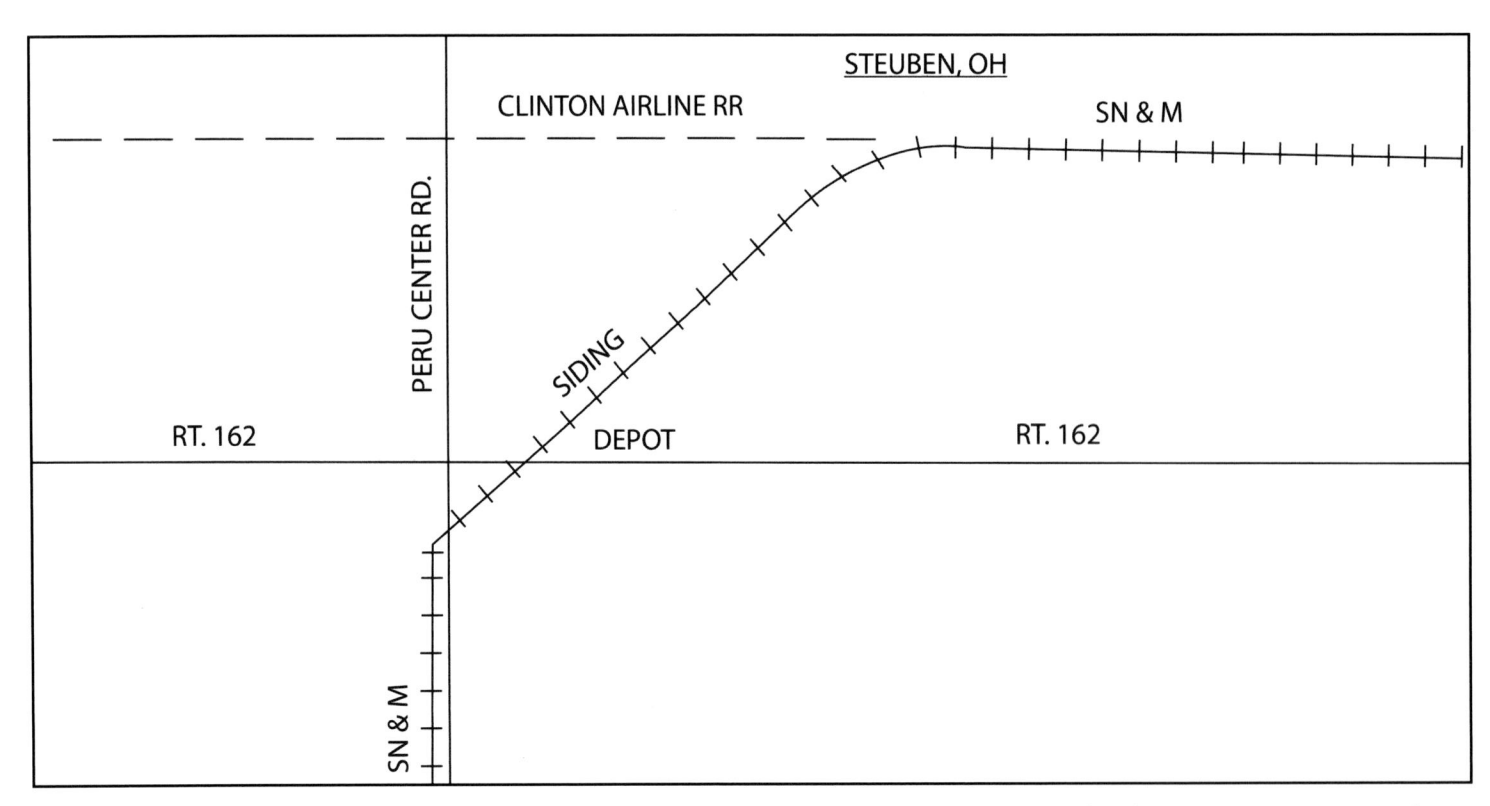

STEUBEN, OH

[Map showing CLINTON AIRLINE RR, SN & M, PERU CENTER RD., RT. 162, SIDING, DEPOT]

Steuben was interesting. The SN&M angled northeast to pick up the old Clinton Air Line roadbed. The Clinton Line was constructed through here in about 1853. The big ridge remained so the SN&M used it where they could. The depot was on the east side of the SN&M and was replaced once. The 2nd structure exists today as a residence.

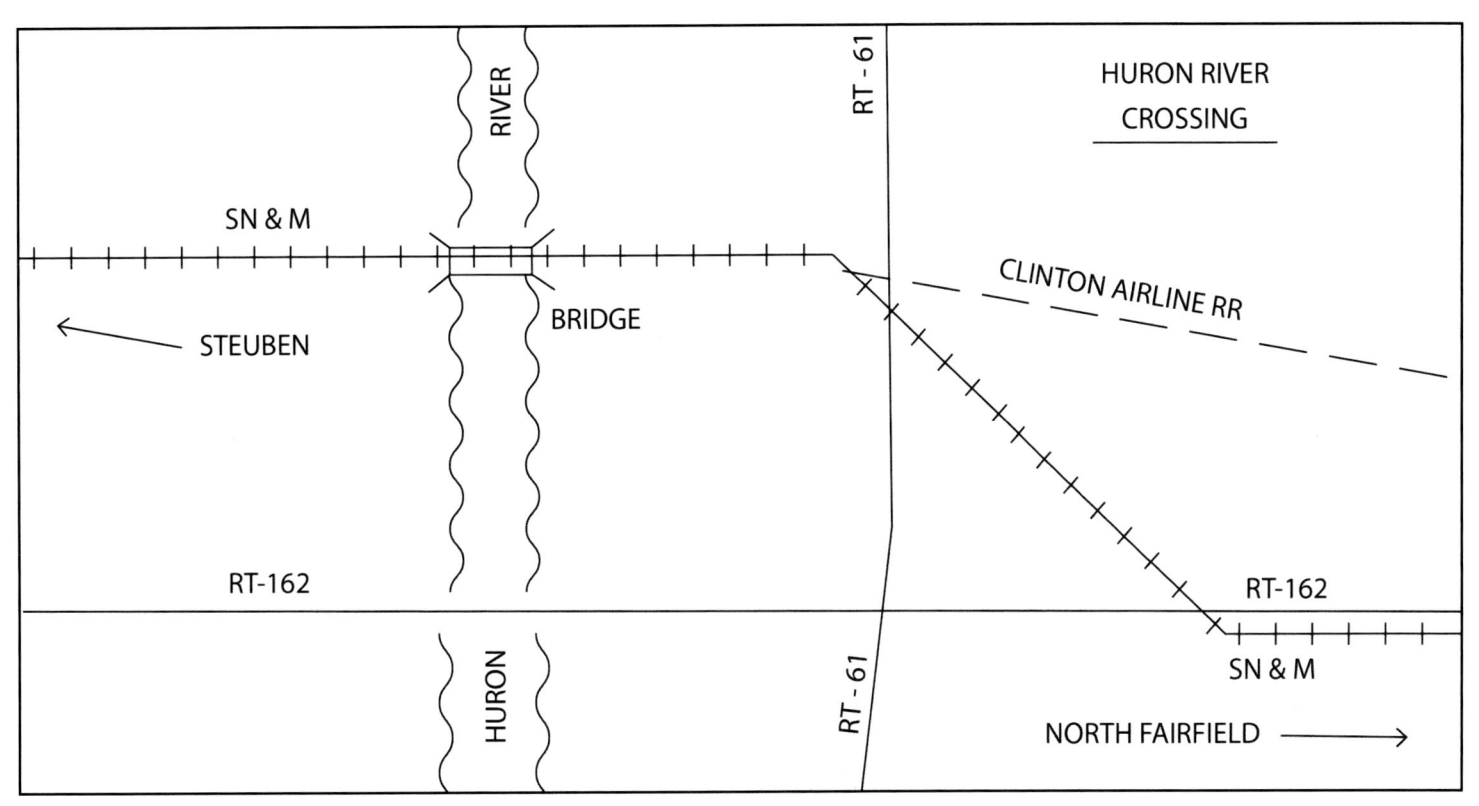

East of Steuben the SN&M went over the Huron River and then came down off the Clinton Line before Rt. 61. It climbed a big hill to cross Route 61 at grade. It then struck southeast and picked up the south side of Rt. 162.

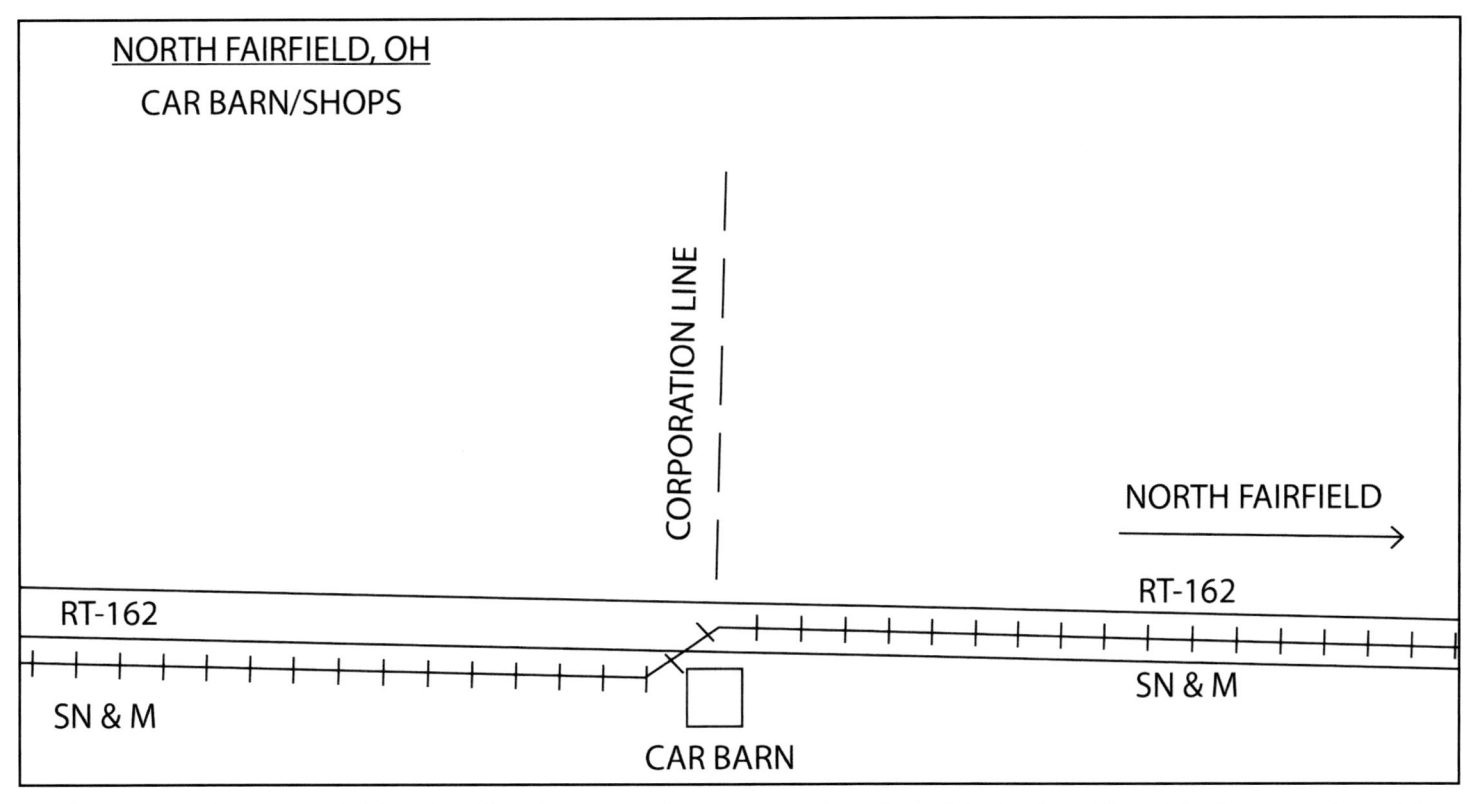

On the west side of North Fairfield, at the village limits, was the car barn and small repair/paint shop. The original structure burned in 1914 and another structure replaced that in 1915.

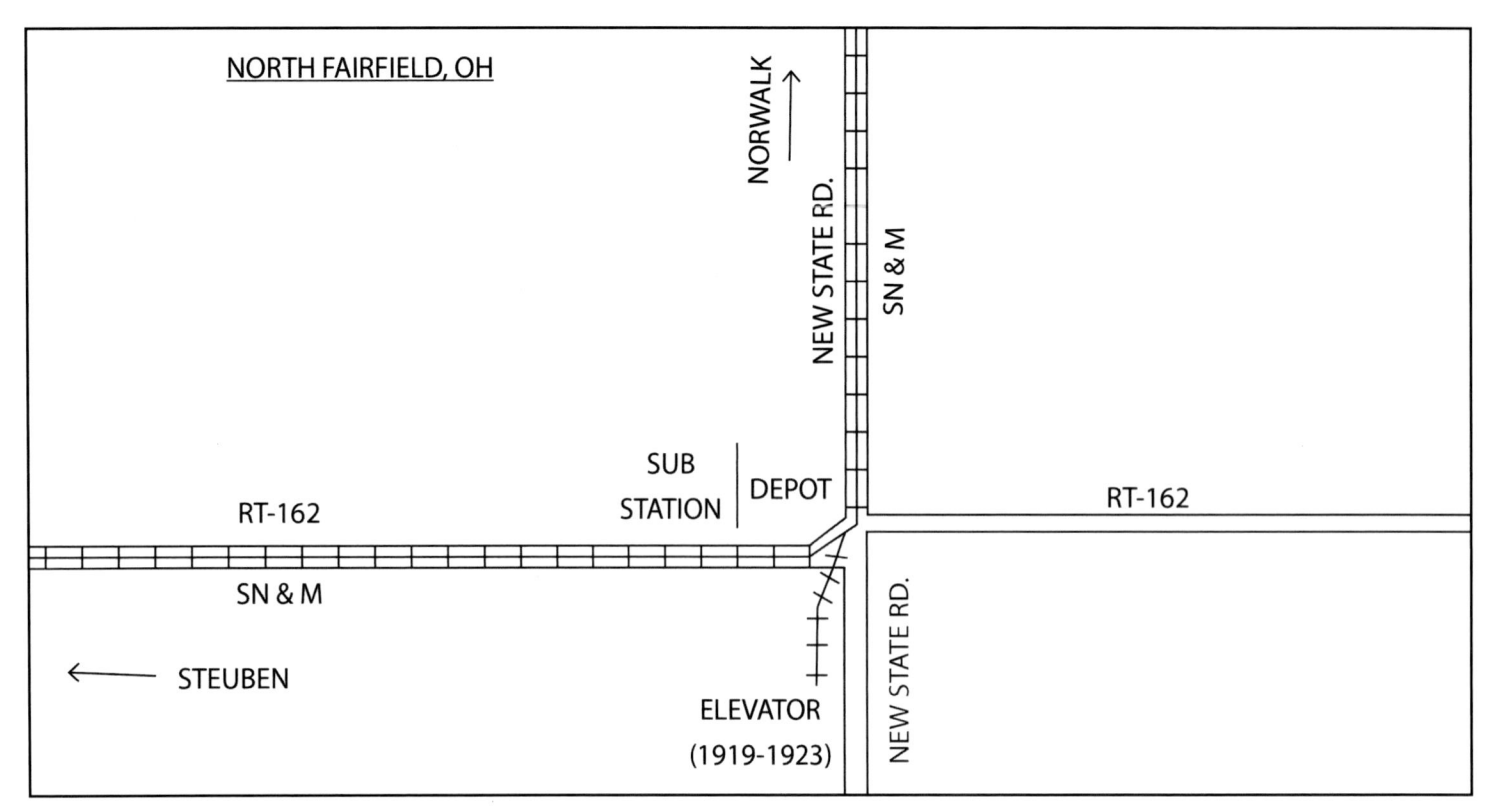

North Fairfield was the SN&M's "headquarters" so to speak. The depot and substation together were on the northwest corner of the square. The Elevator and Mill were later served by the SN&M beginning in 1919. Due to the loss of service after the SN&M was abandoned and the Norwalk & Shelby RR formed, the Elevator moved to Boughtonville in 1923. The track layout was relatively simple: it ran down the middle of the street and wrapped around the curve at the square and continued north.

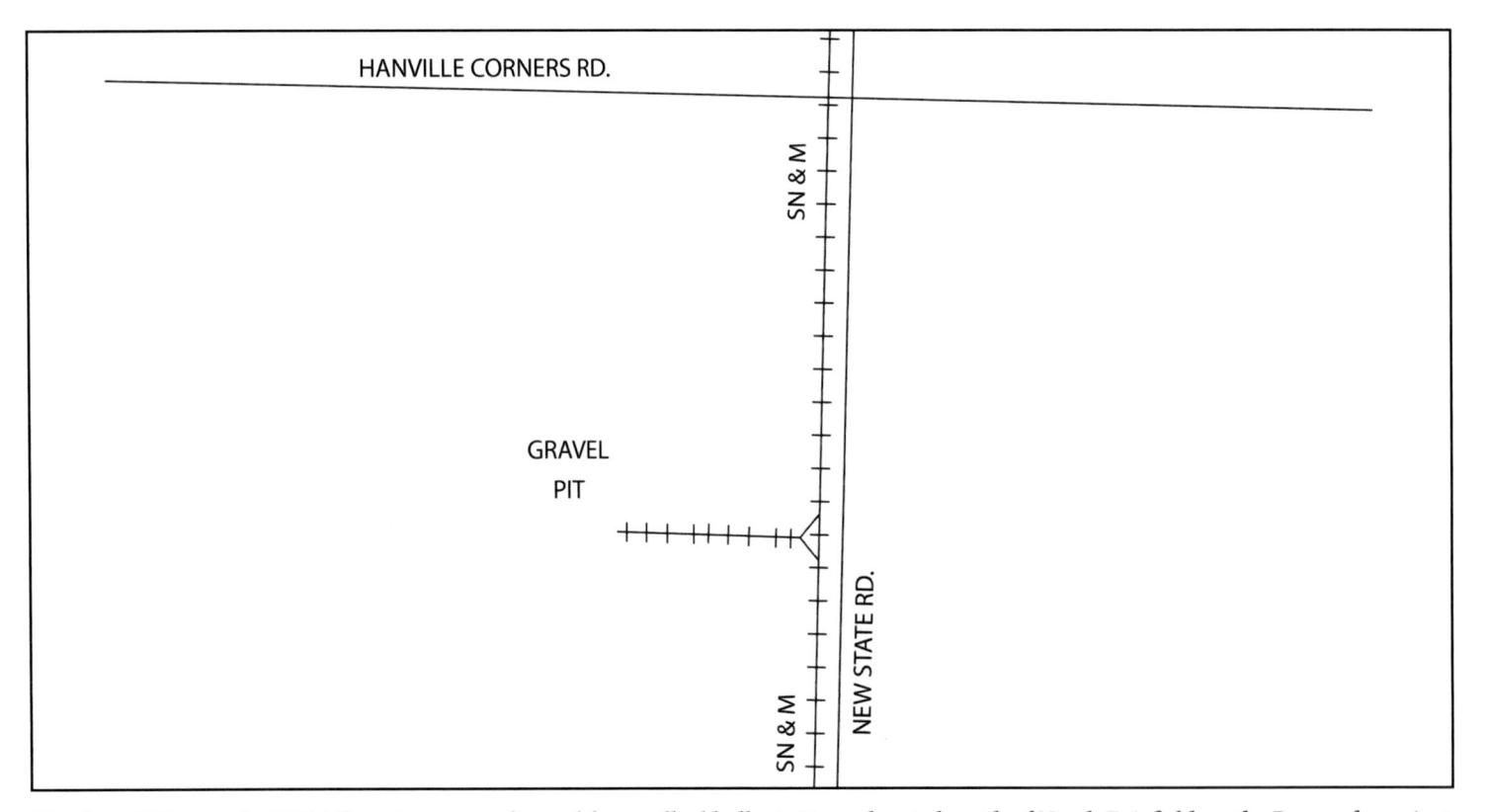

The Gravel Pit was the SN&M's main source of gravel for roadbed ballast. It was located north of North Fairfield on the Burras farm, just south of Hanville Corners. The original siding ran into the pit while the wye arrangement was finished in November of 1905.

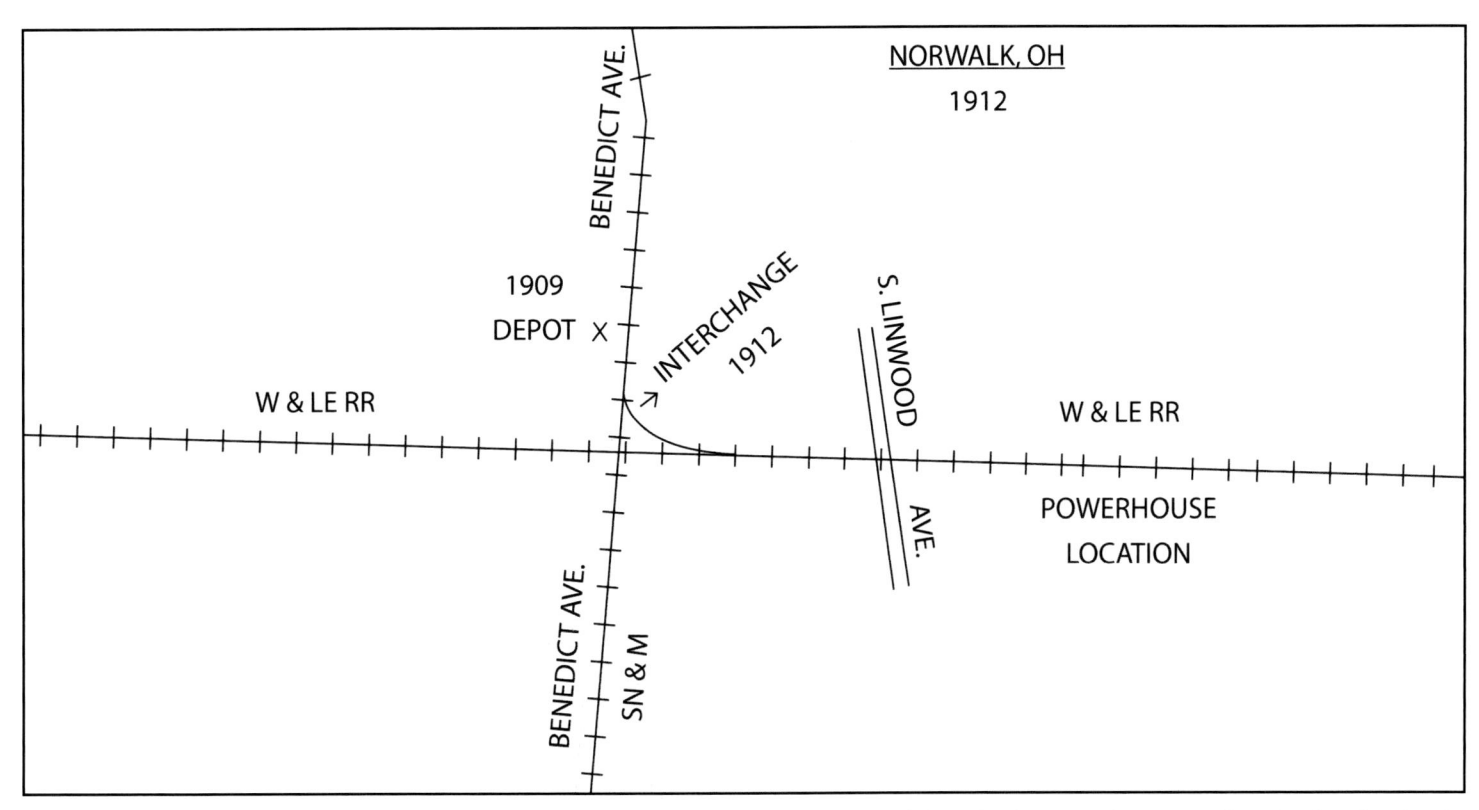

The powerhouse in Norwalk was located east of Benedict Avenue on the south side of the Wheeling & Lake Erie Railroad. The Cleveland Southwestern & Columbus Railway began selling power to the SN&M on July 16, 1910 from this powerhouse. The Wheeling & Lake Erie connection track was completed in 1912. The SN&M depot moved to 46 Benedict in March of 1909.

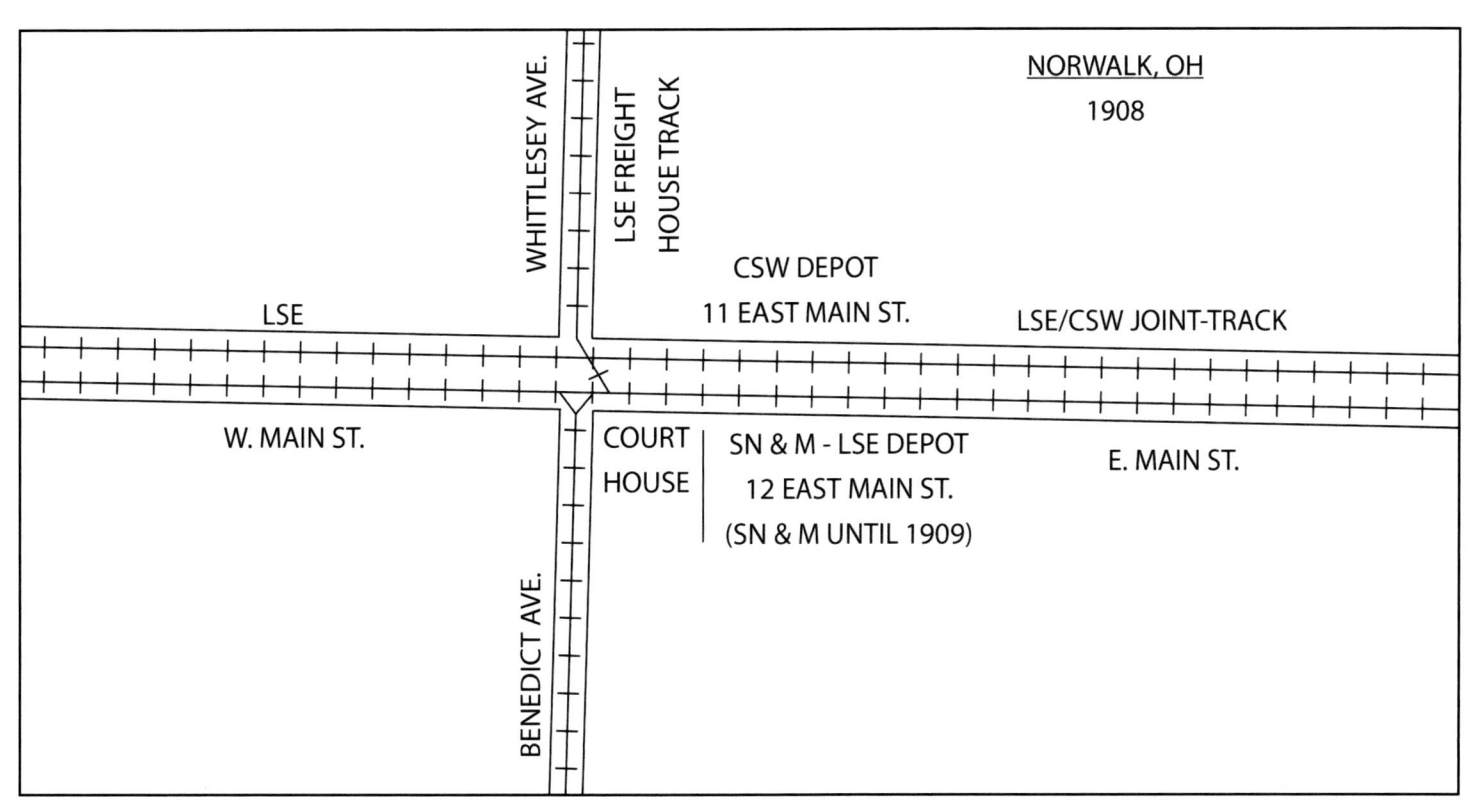

Norwalk in 1908. A simplified map of Norwalk prior to the 1909 SN&M waiting room/depot move to Benedict is shown. The SN&M came up from the south on Benedict and had a wye with the Lake Shore Electric and that's where the SN&M's ownership ended. The cars ran on LSE tracks east to 12 East Main Street where they shared facilities with the LSE. The CSW depot was across the street originally at 11 East Main. The LSE and CSW depots both moved over the years.

PART IV
THE MANSFIELD SHORT LINE RAILROAD

The story of the Mansfield Short Line Railroad is rather fascinating. This little-known "railroad" has history in Shelby, Mansfield, and Lucas. Conceived by a con-man named Charles French, many area investors put money into this venture that resulted in a railroad grade without rails. The frenzy of investor money was spurred by the railroad and interurban craze that was happening in the 1890s. Even Shelby planned to be a "grand railroad center," projecting itself to have trade and travel at levels of that of New York City! At any rate, this lonely grade ran from Shelby to Mansfield and was built quite substantially. For years the right-of-way could been seen, but time is slowly eroding it. Parts of it still remain. The remnants are a mystery to some, and are sometimes even confused with the Mansfield and Shelby Electric interurban. Historians call these types of railroads "paper railroads."

Charles French – The Dynamite Man

The story really begins with a man by the name of Charles French. He was born near the village of Wakeman, Ohio, in 1862, and was one of six children in a family living on a farm. This farm became very important to the story because this is where he learned to use dynamite by charging stumps on the property for removal. French then began working in the employ of several stone quarries around Erie County and Lake Erie. He became very skilled with dynamite and was well-known. For example, he experimented with, and perfected, underwater charges. He was so involved in the stone business that it is said he had his own boat to take up reef rock near Marblehead. Later, he actually formed his own company which would lay the foundation for of his presence in Richland County: He purchased a large area of land south of Sandusky along the Baltimore and Ohio Railroad for the purpose of operating a limestone quarry. A mill was constructed there to process the limestone and the company was known as the Sandusky Stone Company.

Charles French: The Dynamite Man (History of Richland County, Ohio)

Paul White's History – Charles French – The Back Story

Genius, bumbler, persuader, imposter, financial wizard and embezzler were some of the terms used in describing the almost legendary Charlie French whose spurious activities began in Mansfield during the spring of 1889, and continued through the first decade of the 1900s.

To say Charles W. French was a controversial figure of local history would be grossly understating the situation. To some he was a schemer; to others he was a dreamer. It all depended on whether the point of view came from a victim of French's promotions, or whether the observer based his opinion on the benefits promised by French's proposals. The former lost his shirt; the latter quickly became disillusioned.

Charlie learned to out-slicker the city slickers. Born on a farm in Huron County near Wakeman on Sept. 2, 1862, he came from Connecticut stock which dated back to the early seaboard settlers. At 11 years of age, he could load and stack 44 acres of grain along side any man. He was kind to animals. He domesticated wild chipmunks and; he galloped to the village on a spirited horse without using so much as a lead rope, guiding the animal with the pressure of his knees on its flanks.

He was a sensitive child, deeply affected by the loss of his mother when he was 14 years of age. He used neither liquor, tobacco nor participated in a private life from which a good woman would shrink. As a child he was frail and very shy due to severe stammering which afflicted him. His stammering was so serious that it was difficult to understand his speech.

Shunned by other children because of this defect, Charlie turned to books, particularly history, for consolation. He became steeped so deeply in history that he envisioned himself actually living the great moments of the past. One writer said of French, "A shy, nervous boy, dressed in home-made clothes, grew up under the shadow of characters (of history) that have enabled human life in all ages."

French, as a youth, had almost no social life. Attempts to associate with his peers resulted in painful experiences. It is told that at one revival in Wakeman a zealous church woman asked him, "My boy, are you prepared for death?" French stammeringly replied "Yes, I would be willing to die if I thought I could then talk with William of Orange for a few minutes."

At 16, French started to attend debating societies held in the various Huron County school districts. To his surprise, when addressing an audience, he lost his stammering and became a fairly persuasive public speaker.

His first job away from the farm at 19 was cutting stove wood during the winter of 1881-82. He again returned to the farm during the summer of 1882, and in the fall of that year he first became acquainted with the use of dynamite. He used it to blow stumps on the farm woodlot.

Dynamite and Charlie French became synonymous from then on. He seemed to have an uncanny skill in handling high explosives of which at that time, little was known. He became proficient in setting just the right charge to accomplish work which otherwise would require many man-hours of hard labor. He applied his acquired skill in the sandstone and limestone quarries of the Sandusky and Lake Erie island area where he would set charges to strip the materials from the quarries quickly and economically.

After introducing the use of dynamite in the quarries, he experimented with underwater charges. It is said that Charlie French could fire single charges containing a ton of dynamite to strip stone and building materials from the quarries. Money started to roll Charlie's way but then the first in a series of financial difficulties occurred; these reversals plagued him for the remainder of his life. At 22 he went bankrupt for a debt of $20,000. This was a small fortune in those days.

French demonstrated a quick rebound from his financial depths, as he would so many times throughout the remainder of his life. In a short period of time he again acquired considerable property in Sandusky. To rise out of financial disaster he applied his inventive genius in constructing a novel work barge for taking up reef rock off the shores of the Erie islands near Marblehead. Experienced seamen of the area, upon examining his barge, declared it an utter failure. However, Charlie brought up the reef rock, constructed a mill for crushing the limestone rock into ballast which had commercial value in the days of the sailing vessels. This plant was located four miles south of Sandusky on the Baltimore and Ohio Railroad. Even before the mill was completed, he organized his first of many companies, the Sandusky Stone Co.

Charlie French was now underway with his dream of a great financial empire. He looked around for other worlds to conquer. His search centered on the area approximately 60 miles south of Sandusky and there he decided to establish his next facility.

In the spring of 1889, French and his associates bought a tract of sandstone quarry land near Lucas, in Richland County, just a few miles southeast of Mansfield on the Pennsylvania Railroad line. Thus, Charles W. French came to Mansfield to build a legend around himself during the following 30 years.

Lucas – The Baker Stone Company and the Real Story

Meanwhile in Lucas, Ohio, a stone quarry was being mined for sandstone just west of the village. Hiram Baker, a local landowner, owned the entire quarry area. In 1883, he established the Baker Stone Company and did a fairly sporadic business in the years 1883-1885. The operations were quite successful overall and stone was being shipped out every month. The stone was unique in the fact that some of it was dark red while other parts of the quarry were pure white. The stone was good enough to be used for the Reformatory in Mansfield, as well as the Balliet Bridge in Lexington. This is where Charles French enters the story. Although he was vice president of his company, he was the front man and did all of the speaking and negotiations for the company. In early 1889, he approached the businessmen of Lucas for the prospect of buying a section or portion of the quarry. The selling point is that he would really improve the business by building all sorts of machinery and by connecting to the Pennsylvania Railroad with a spur track into the quarry. Dr. William S. Mecklem, Professor D. W. Andrews, and Captain S. M. First of Lucas met with Charles French and his representatives and made a deal. The first thing French did was to officially incorporate the entire quarry area. On March 12, 1889, the Baker Stone Company was officially incorporated in Lucas with a capital stock of $25,000. At that time French and Company purchased only a narrow section of the larger quarry along the west edge. This narrow strip was what technically became the Baker Stone Company, while the other, larger section became the Lucas Stone Company. Each were under separate ownership and control although French toyed with the idea of purchasing the entire property.

From the get-go, French seemed to be a con man. Stories abounded of him not paying employees or not paying them on time, dodging bills, and swindling investors. He appeared to be making progress however. In 1889, he started his own railroad venture by forming the Northwestern and Monroe Railroad Company. The railroad company was formed to construct a spur track from the Pennsylvania Railroad into his strip of the quarry. On June 8, 1889, grading began for the spur track. Whether the PRR ever agreed to a switch from their track at this time is unknown. In 1890, French stated that his "railroad" would be extended from Lucas to Mansfield so that all could enjoy the stone from his quarry. He even made his railroad "official." As was the custom of the day, presidents of railroads exchanged courtesy passes with the presidents of other railroads. These passes gave free passage to the holder. French had some magnificently embossed, steel engraved passes made for the Northwestern and Monroe Railroad and sent them to all the large railroad company presidents. He of course received passes for their lines in return. French rode the rails in style as he traveled around the country on his courtesy passes until one day the president of one of the large railroads (unknown) came to the area to ride on French's railroad. Much to his chagrin he found that French's railroad extended about a half mile off the Pennsylvania Railroad mainline up a hill and dead-ended in a sandstone quarry! Word soon got around to the other railroads and French no longer received courtesy passes.

The quarry "set up" at Lucas was a source of confusion for many until it stopped being mined in 1898. Because it was technically one large quarry divided into two properties, the newspapers constantly confused one with the other and even sometimes referred to both collectively. The larger section not owned by French never changed names; it was always the Lucas Stone Company after 1889. French's side changed names often, for swindling purposes.

At any rate, during the first part of the quarry project at Lucas, French married Alberta Walker of Sandusky on June 27, 1890. Alberta Walker was the daughter of the superintendent of the Sandusky Stone Company. On Thanksgiving Day 1888, Mr. Walker had been killed by a dynamite charge in the Sandusky quarry. After marriage, Alberta came to Mansfield with Charles and she was made secretary and book keeper of his Lucas quarry. They had one child together, but unfortunately he died at 4 months of age. Alberta's two younger sisters and her mother lived with them and they later adopted three daughters, living at 42 Sherman Avenue.

The Baker Stone Quarry at Lucas, Ohio, in the 1890s. (Tim Johnson)

The PRR Locomotive

The Northwest and Monroe Railroad Company was finally built and was only the spur track into the quarry (perhaps the shortest railroad in the world). According to newspaper reports on August 27, 1891, French and his gang stole a PRR locomotive from the Mansfield yard. Meanwhile, the gangs tied into the PRR at Lucas by building a switch. When French got back with the steam engine, they pulled it into the spur track and his gangs quickly removed the switch—therefore, he literally stole a PRR locomotive! The PRR figured this out quickly and contacted the sheriff. A group of PRR men, accompanied by Deputy Sheriff Guthrie of Richland County, came down to Lucas to get the locomotive. The PRR men put the temporary switch back in and got the locomotive off the spur track and back to Mansfield. The courts fined French $300, and it is incredibly likely he never paid it. Since the Northwest and Monroe Railroad had no locomotive, this was French's best idea to obtain one. It didn't work.

In 1891, the name of French's side of the quarry was changed to the Monroe Stone Company. The larger, eastern portion remained the Lucas Stone Company. In fact, even through 1895, the properties were still listed as separate (Monroe and Lucas), so it is likely French never even purchased the entire area. In 1896, French formed the Columbia Stone Company but this was likely a "paper name" to avoid some sort of legal trouble involving money. In reality, from 1889 to 1897, French's presence in Richland County was fairly modest, more or less operating the quarry. He liked to convince investors to give him money with no intention of paying them back; he dreamed big, but had no intention to fork over any of his own money. The following year would be the beginning of French's real presence.

The Mansfield Short Line Railroad (French's Folly)

French's properties became complicated very quickly because he kept "forming" new companies to attract investor money. With the quarry property in place, he could now convince many to lend money. In the spring of 1897, he created what was known as the Mansfield Short Line Railroad or "The Short Line." The proposal began in Mansfield because for years Mansfield businessmen had felt snubbed because the New York Central's Big Four route had bypassed Mansfield through Shelby and Crestline to the west. French's proposal was attractive. He would build a railroad line from the NYC in Shelby, directly to the business and industrial districts of Mansfield. As a further attraction, he would continue the line over to Lucas and his own quarry. Investor money came flowing in and he was able to do a lot of cheap construction and grading to fool the investors into thinking some progress was being made. Because a lot of grading was completed and a lot of talk was done—with no results—for years after French left the area, the Mansfield Short Line was affectionately known as "French's Folly." The Northwest and Monroe Railroad was still a separate company.

In 1897, French hired surveyors to survey a route from Shelby to Mansfield. The original survey left Shelby on the east side of the NYC tracks at Main Street, and continued south paralleling the Big Four for a short distance, before aiming southeast at the end of Summit Street. It then went straight southeast to the B&O crossing on Mickey Road, and then picking up the east side of the B&O all the way to Mansfield. The Mickey Road/B&O crossing was known as Fletcher's Crossing due to the Fletcher Farm on the east side of the B&O there (B&O east to Dowd's Elementary location). With his tactics in an unlimited supply, he formed yet another company called the Richland & Mahoning Railroad that would extend east of Mansfield to Akron, Canton, Youngstown, etc. This company was incorporated on May 25, 1898, for a capital stock of $150,000. The reason this is important is that he convinced Mansfield investors to dump even more money into the Mansfield Short Line because it was part of this larger Richland & Mahoning Railroad system.

Investors were getting increasingly frustrated with French because no rails had been laid between Shelby and Mansfield, despite some sparse grading having been done. He hired the Crouch Construction Company of Rapid City, SD, to do initial grading work. All through 1898 and into 1899, he stalled on the project. Meanwhile, he gave up on the Lucas quarry idea. He was running now

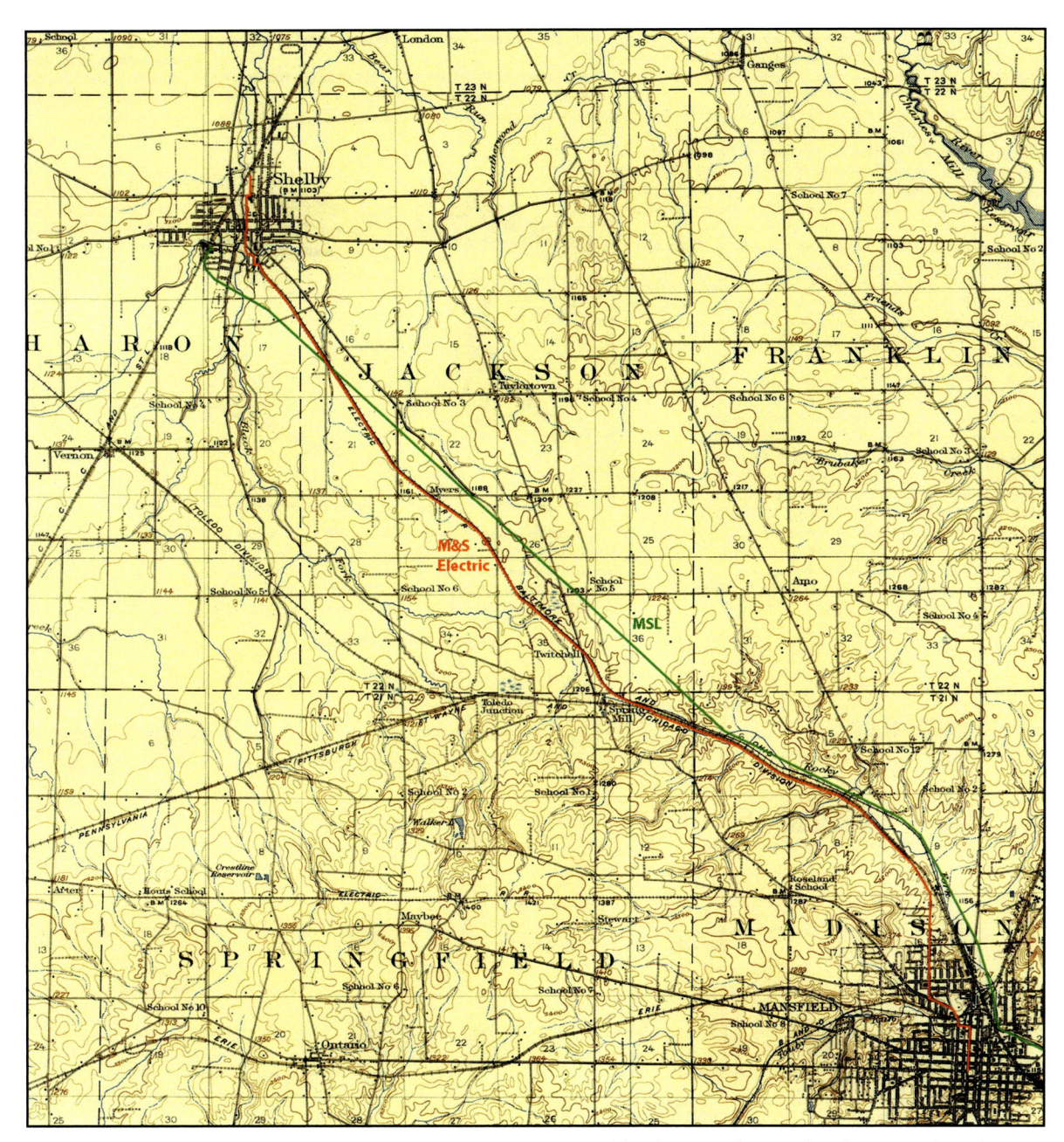

The Mansfield Short Line was graded in its entirety as indicated by the green line in the above quadrangle map. For comparison, the M&S electric line is shown in red. (Courtesy of the USGS)

with the Richland and Mahoning Railroad "empire," as he called it. The quarry in Lucas really had little use anymore, so both companies sold their parts to T. A. Parry of Lucas, on April 7, 1898. The Lucas quarry, where this had all begun, was no more. Oddly, the Northwest and Monroe Railroad was still a company.

On December 3, 1899, French made a new survey on part of the MSL RR, between Shelby and Mansfield. The Rogers Farm was located on Mickey Road in Shelby (where the reservoir is located) and the right-of-way went through this farm. He modified the routing by turning it to the south and running arrow-straight to a point along the B&O RR at Spring Mill, just past Leppo Road. It would cross the B&O at grade a few hundred feet south of George Hawk Road. According to reports this would cut off ½ mile from the original survey to Mansfield. The entire survey was completed on December 28, 1899, and the officials of the MSL took a brief walking tour of the property. Many Mansfield businessmen had helped French secure and purchase the right-of-way.

In the early part of 1900, Charles French hired a Sandusky attorney, named H. L. Peeke. No doubt for the protection of French himself, all of the property went into H. L. Peeke's name. Together they issued subscription notes and lobbied for more money in both Shelby and Mansfield, from January to March of 1900. During the remainder of 1900, land was purchased piecemeal and often involved law suits and condemnation proceedings. Despite that, on August 16, 1900, French announced his grand plans for the Shelby "terminal," as he called it. Charles French called the *Shelby Daily Globe* that day and stated that the Richland and Mahoning Railroad he was building would soon absorb the MSL; Shelby would be the western terminal of a through-route from Shelby to Youngstown and Pittsburgh. No doubt the Vanderbilts of the NYC fame would purchase his line and use it as a coal feeder to the Big Four. There would be freight and passenger depots at the West Main Street/NYC crossing where the terminal would be located. He mentioned that a grand union passenger depot would be built in Mansfield, just south of the crossing of the Pennsylvania Railroad and the B&O. By this time, investors were growing weary because he had literally laid no rails.

It must be mentioned that no farmer in the area had to give up as much land as A. J. Twitchell, who owned the farm on the north side of the B&O tracks on Leppo Road, east of Spring Mill. Originally, a big farm with no railroads the B&O cut through first, followed by the Pennsylvania Railroad. The Mansfield and Shelby interurban line had been projected to follow the south side of the PRR through the property, and now the court awarded a strip of land to Charles French for his MSL. A. J. Twitchell had to sell French the strip for $2300 on August 24, 1900.

Substantial Grading Begins

Although some grading had already been done here and there by the Crouch Construction Company and the J. E. Kerr Construction Company, some serious grading was done in the summer of 1900 by another contractor, the C. E. Loss and Company of Chicago. They dug a big cut at Springmill and did the grading throughout that entire area. On September 12, 1900, he hired yet another contractor, this time from Republic, Ohio. This contractor had been doing work with the Baltimore and Ohio Railroad and would be on French's property by September 18 with 25 teams. They began on the Mansfield end and did some grading and structural removal in the flats. At this point, grading was being done on both ends of the line. French's Lucas Construction Company was formed around this time too.

Gamble Street Overpass

On October 11, 1900, French attended the Shelby City Council meeting (the same meeting Reid Carpenter of the M&S interurban line attended). He was there to ask permission and to be granted a franchise to construct an overhead bridge over South Gamble Street, just south of Grace St. He wished the bridge to clear Gamble by 13 feet. The city council thought it should be 15 feet. French contended that to add an additional 2 feet it would cost $7,000 and was not possible. He offered that the bridge would be very fine, even boarded on the bottom to prevent cinders and other debris from falling. If city council wouldn't relent on the 15 foot clearance, he stated he would have to put in a grade crossing and that would not be as safe. City council adjourned, having made no decision yet, but would soon decide on the matter.

The decision did come quickly, and on October 12, 1900, the Shelby City Council granted the MSL a franchise to build an overhead bridge over South Gamble Street, at a height of 13'10." The bridge would also have to have the floor already mentioned, and the company would have to construct sidewalks under the bridge, on each side of Gamble. Needless to say, the bridge was never constructed. Interestingly, the street ordinance was passed, too. Basically, the route was to leave the Main Street crossing with the Big Four and sort of parallel the Big Four to a point just past Summit

Street and then arc southeast to Mansfield. The article read that from Main Street the line would parallel the Big Four for 1500 feet before turning southeast. On November 3, 1900, Mansfield City Council granted the MSL their city franchise. As will be explained later the right-of-way in Mansfield began 100 feet east of North Main Street (Rt. 13) on Longview Avenue, and followed a generally southeast direction through the "flats" of Mansfield.

On November 17, 1900, French slightly changed his plans in Shelby. The terminal or passenger station would be the Shelby Tube Works Office, north of South Street, on the east side of the Big Four. The building would be purchased by French and his offices would be located in the building, along with the passenger waiting room and ticket office. Obviously, this never occurred. But that didn't stop him from constructing his grade. As will be explained later, the entire grade from Shelby to Mansfield was actually constructed but very piecemeal. It was constructed here and there, in separate parts, and by several contractors. Therefore the newspapers had difficulty in tracking progress. Enough grading progress had been completed however, that when Reid Carpenter of the Citizen's Electric Railway, Light, and Power Company was planning his interurban route to Shelby he considered using the Mansfield Short Line grade rather than build his own. This also lent insight into the fact that Carpenter (and perhaps other business owners) by now did not believe that French's line would be successful.

French claimed he would purchase the Shelby Tube Works Office and use it as a freight and passenger depot. The Tube Works Office sat on the east side of the Big Four Railroad north of South Street. (Shelby Museum of History)

Battle With the Pennsylvania Railroad in Mansfield

Construction crews had been in Mansfield since November 13, 1900, but a big project was planned for November 30. French, growing desperate to secure more funding and to get his railroad constructed, sent his construction crews to Mansfield and ordered the right-of-way constructed through. French was very serious and desperate so he sent both the Crouch Construction Company and the C. E. Loss and Company; construction foreman C. D. Crouch of Chicago was in charge. To complete the grading the Pennsylvania Railroad spur tracks along Newman would have to be crossed. French's MSL crossed Orange Street just east of Beymiller, followed by the Rocky Fork, the

This photo was taken from the water tower at the Chicago Handle Bar Company on South Street in Shelby. The Tube Works Office is on the extreme right. With a keen eye French's right-of-way can be seen between the fence running along the center, and the Big Four railroad tracks. (Shelby Museum of History)

Eclipse Stove Works siding of the PRR, and finally Newman. When the PRR caught wind that the construction companies were coming with crews of men, they summoned their own men to come and stop them. Section Foreman P. J. Adams of the PRR summoned track crews from Crestline, Loudonville, and other places, to Mansfield. The PRR first retaliated by building a new spur track through the MSL grade. The PRR also piled ties, dirt, rails, etc. in the way of the MSL crews. The PRR had summoned hundreds of workers to come and stop the MSL. A big fight also broke out and while many punches were thrown, there were no serious injuries. During this battle an injunction was sought against the PRR by the MSL to stop the building of the new spur track to block the grading. Judge Wolfe granted the injunction and the PRR could not build the new spur. The men from both sides walked away for the night, after the fighting had stopped and the injunction served.

The next day, at 10:00 AM, , the battle took up where it had left off the previous evening. More punches and dirt were thrown throughout the early part of the afternoon. The PRR continued building little sections of track to keep getting in the way of the MSL grade. On December 3, 1900, the Pennsylvania Railroad, Erie Railroad, and Baltimore & Ohio Railroad—the three railroads of Mansfield—all filed a joint-injunction against the MSL. They stated that the MSL was insolvent and had no legal right to cross any railroad at grade. Bad news was handed down in court in November. French tried to consolidate the Northwest and Monroe Railroad at Lucas with his Mansfield Short Line Railroad and was denied because the county had liens on the Lucas property. Litigation with the PRR in December didn't get anywhere, either. Time was running out for French and the Mansfield Short Line Railroad.

In 1901, French tried some other strategies to regain investor trust. He declared on January 14, 1901, that the line from the crossing with the B&O at George Hawk Road, southeast of Shelby, would be double-tracked. Furthermore, he claimed that the B&O would abandon their line from that point to Mansfield in favor of joining his MSL RR there because it was a much more direct route. On January 17, 1901, he went back to Mansfield and discussed the Union Depot idea again. Surprisingly, on January 29, 1901, French's crews actually began laying rail at Spring Mill that had been brought in on cars on the Pennsylvania Railroad. In October of 1900 he had removed the rails at the Lucas quarry and these were used as well. Obviously, there weren't enough rails to be laid from there to either Mansfield or Shelby; likely this was to impress upon investors that he was serious and could make progress. Later that year it was said he laid a short section of rail on the west side of George Hawk Road southeast of Shelby for the same reasons.

Believe it or not, French did purchase a steam engine and painted it as Chicago Short Line. Obviously it was never operated, at least not by any of his companies. (National Archives, College Park, MD)

The Chicago Short Line Railroad

On February 4, 1901, French organized what was called the Chicago Short Line Railroad, or CSL for short. Apparently, he had formed another "paper railroad" after the MSL was formed that wasn't discussed much but was called the Shelby and New Washington Railroad, running from Shelby to the Northern Ohio Railroad in New Washington (later the AC&Y). Whether this was ever discussed with investors or not, it was being discussed now. French merged his Mansfield Short Line Railroad with his Shelby and New Washington Railroad. The premise was that Chicago could be reached after connecting to the Northern Ohio Railroad at New Washington and taking that to Carey, the NYC to Findlay, the Findlay, Fort Wayne, and Western to Fort Wayne, and finally the NKP to Chicago. Meanwhile French's Richland and Mahoning property in the Akron area underwent a reorganization. Officers for the Chicago Short Line were elected as follows: C. W. French, president; A. A. Purman, vice president; and W. S. Cappellar, secretary. The CSL was bonded for $2,765,000. After this the remaining sections of the MSL route were finished being constructed. The grading was done from the Shelby Tube Works office all the way to Mansfield to a point just shy of Illinois Avenue along the Rocky Fork. The fill and approaches were done on all stream crossings and it was even reported that some of the concrete was poured for small bridges. The rail remained at Spring Mill, but no more was laid and this is the most construction that would ever be done. The CSL was declared to be the "southern route"—and the Richland and Mahoning would be the "northern route" and each would meet at New Washington. This was nothing but a smokescreen for investors.

The Past Catches Up

Eventually, the past caught up to Charles French. Back on October 6, 1898, J. E. Kerr of the Kerr

Construction Company had already sued the MSL for $774.10 owed for grading work. The court ruled on May 2, 1900, that the MSL owed Kerr $789.14 plus court costs. If it were not paid within 10 days, the court would place a lien on the property. The debt was never paid and Kerr sued again. On April 18, 1901, Kerr et. al. asked that the road be foreclosed or put into receivership. The judge, however, ordered the line foreclosed and sold. Seeing the writing on the wall, officers Huntington Brown and W. S. Cappellar resigned on July 22, 1901. Because French was in court quite a bit from April 1901 to April 1902, it is said that at a court hearing on March 24, 1902, it was learned he was a talented musician. Due to being anxious and deeply troubled over the court hearing, he played quite a fine tune on his jews harp. This was another idiosyncrasy of French.

The auction did not occur until April 28, 1902, due to numerous other lawsuits along the way. The MSL section from Shelby to Mansfield was appraised at $1200 but sold for $1000 much to the surprise of the citizens. Judge Brucker bid and won, but he quickly transferred the deeds over to his assistant D. W. Cummins. This raised suspicion because Cummins was a trustee for some of French's creditors.

French's eccentric behavior continued when on December 6, 1902, he was seen dressed as a cowboy. This didn't help his financial matters. Cummins paid no debt off and French had been run out of town by investors and creditors, and so the road was forced back into foreclosure and another sale was to take place. On Saturday February 11, 1905, the big foreclosure sale finally took place for the MSL section. The road this time was appraised at $9000, and the sale included the franchises, right-of-way, ties, and rails. H. L. Peeke of Sandusky, French's attorney, purchased the MSL at the Richland County Court House for $10,000. The farmers along the route were more than willing to purchase their land back for a very small fee. Peeke didn't sell the rails that had been laid at Springmill long ago until February 8, 1907. The MSL and CSL were no more.

Charles French Epilogue

French had many run-ins with the law over the next 10-15 years, but the most significant was in 1921, when he was actually arrested in Chicago after having been accused of being involved in a bond robbery. He was released on bond in exchange for telling federal investigators about all of his swindles. It was likely one of his smooth speeches that he so often used on investors that got him out of this legal trouble. Not much was heard from French again. It should be mentioned that during this investigation in Chicago a warrant was issued for H. L. Peeke's arrest. It does not appear either man served jail time. Many remembered Charles French for years in Richland County as the con man who played the jews harp and constructed French's Folly.

Following the Mansfield Short Line Railroad Today

Believe it or not, this long forgotten entity can still, to this day, be traced and examined. The last shovel was lifted in 1901 contributing to its construction, but it was constructed heavily. Although Father Time has eroded much, something still remains if one knows where to look. This guide will explain everything. Keep in mind the most difficult section is from the Big Four Railroad in Shelby southeast to the Black Fork. A considerable amount has been erased by new home development.

Grading began in Shelby at the site of the old Steel Tube Office. For some unknown reason it was located across the Big Four tracks from the Tuby. It was located north of South Street, along the Big Four, on the alley south of the stream. It is long gone. At any rate the grading was done about 1500 feet to the south and parallel to the Big Four. At Summit Street, at the dead end, it began to curve southeast. It crossed Earl Avenue just west of the end of asphalt, and then curved harder heading to Walnut. To pin-point the crossing location of Walnut, it is now the fourth home on the west side of the street north of Ray. It then crossed Ray just west of where Ray dead ends at the alley. The last difficulty will be pinpointing where it crossed South Gamble and where the big grand bridge was to be located. The right-of-way ran partially through the lot of 114 South Gamble Street and continued straight southeast across the Black Fork. 114 South Gamble is the last home on the street heading south before the cemetery drive is reached.

Heading southeast out of the development the Black Fork is reached. Hiking back to the crossing is well worth the effort as a very large dirt embankment remains on the west side. The east side embankment was eradicated years ago when the original reservoir was constructed in the flat along the Black Fork here. This original reservoir was filled in 1999, and is now simply a grass lot.

Continuing on, it is not worth exploring the Rogers farm and the split of the original and new alignments. That farm today is entirely occupied by the current reservoir. More importantly, the original alignment was never constructed, only the new alignment was built; therefore, the guide follows only the alignment that was actually graded. The MSL crossed Mickey Road immediately east of Riverview Drive. The crossing "hump" is still in place on Mickey Road and motorists today drive over it unaware of its history.

The MSL ran behind the old car dealership on the southwest corner of Mickey and Martin, and the big building is angled on the MSL property line. There is no evidence where Martin Drive crosses the MSL, but behind the old AMF building there is. The MSL would have crossed Martin Drive a few feet south of Shelby Printing and through part of the AMF building. It would have ran southeast of AMF out of the southeast corner of the building and going to that point, one can clearly see the right-of-way beyond as a tree row picks up the grade, heading southeast to George Hawk Road.

At George Hawk Road we have an absolute transportation history phenomenon. The first railroad line in Richland County was the Sandusky, Mansfield, and Newark Railroad that later became the B&O. The line ran from Newark to Mansfield, then to Sandusky via Shelby; this is the same railroad at George Hawk Road. The interurban line which parallels the B&O through this area was one of the first true interurbans in the country, having been constructed in 1901. Therefore, we have a railroad, an interurban, and a paper railroad that was graded, all in the same location! Rumors abounded that French would construct an overhead bridge here over the B&O (interurban wasn't here yet), but obviously that did not happen.

Continuing southeast, development has been a little cruel to the MSL. However, if one drives south on Rock Road the MSL can be spotted. There is a farm house on the west side of Rock Road just before reaching the B&O (Ashland Railway). The MSL clipped the northeast corner of the lot. Additionally, when Ohio Power built their high tension lines, they placed a tower in the field to the west, directly on the MSL grade.

The line more or less remained on a southeasterly direction. Rebecca Lane literally parallels the MSL. The backs of the lots on the west side of Rebecca Lane parallel the MSL property line. The grade then crosses Myers Road exactly where Rebecca meets the road. It crosses Oesch Lane where the second driveway is located south of Myers. There is no physical evidence but it crosses Rt. 39 just north of Cornell Abraxas. It then crosses Plymouth-Springmill Road just north of the Plymouth-Springmill/Rt. 39 intersection and then went across Amoy West Road. Home development has again erased traces in this area. The MSL crosses Amoy West Road at the first driveway on the south side of the road adjacent to a tree row on the north side of the road. Still on the same angle to the southeast the MSL next crosses Spring Mill North Road just north of the road's S-curve. Up ahead it goes through a thick woods and then crosses Cairns Road just west of Leppo Road and then immediately crosses Leppo Road to the south at the old Twitchell Farm. The roadbed is constructed quite substantially at this point and this is likely where French had laid his rail.

From here the MSL picks up the north side of the B&O for the most part. At the Old Bowman Street however the Pennsylvania Railroad and B&O curve hard to the south to Mansfield but the MSL kept going on its own tangent, crossing Longview Avenue exactly 100 feet east of North Main Street (Rt. 13) next to the BP gas station.

From here the grade was constructed through the railroad area. It crossed the Erie Railroad directly adjacent to the dead-end Spring Street and then turned south to parallel the Rocky Fork. It crossed Orange Street just west of Beymiller and then entered the PRR battle site. Immediately after crossing the Rocky Fork on the west side of Newman it abruptly turned southeast and picked up the south side of the Rocky Fork. It paralleled the Rocky Fork to East Fifth/Rt. 39 and then it sort of "bowed" away from the road running directly to the East Fifth/Park Avenue East intersection. It continued to parallel the Rocky Fork to the back of the Tucker Brothers Auto Wrecking yard where grading ended. That's as far as French and his MSL ever got.

Tracing The Lucas Quarry and the Northwestern And Monroe Railroad Company

There isn't much left of the old Lucas quarry. In fact the entire property is private and it isn't recommended to explore. However, it was located west of town off Route 39 on the north side of the road. The spur track crossed Route 39 approximately where the west corporation limit sign is next to a driveway and the spur track went up a short grade here. The entire quarry area was located north of here in the big hill. The spur track connected with the Pennsylvania Railroad directly behind the Lucas Community Center. This is the location of the famous 1891 locomotive theft by French. And that is the state affairs of French's properties in Richland County.

KEY MAPS OF THE MANSFIELD SHORT LINE RAILROAD ROUTE

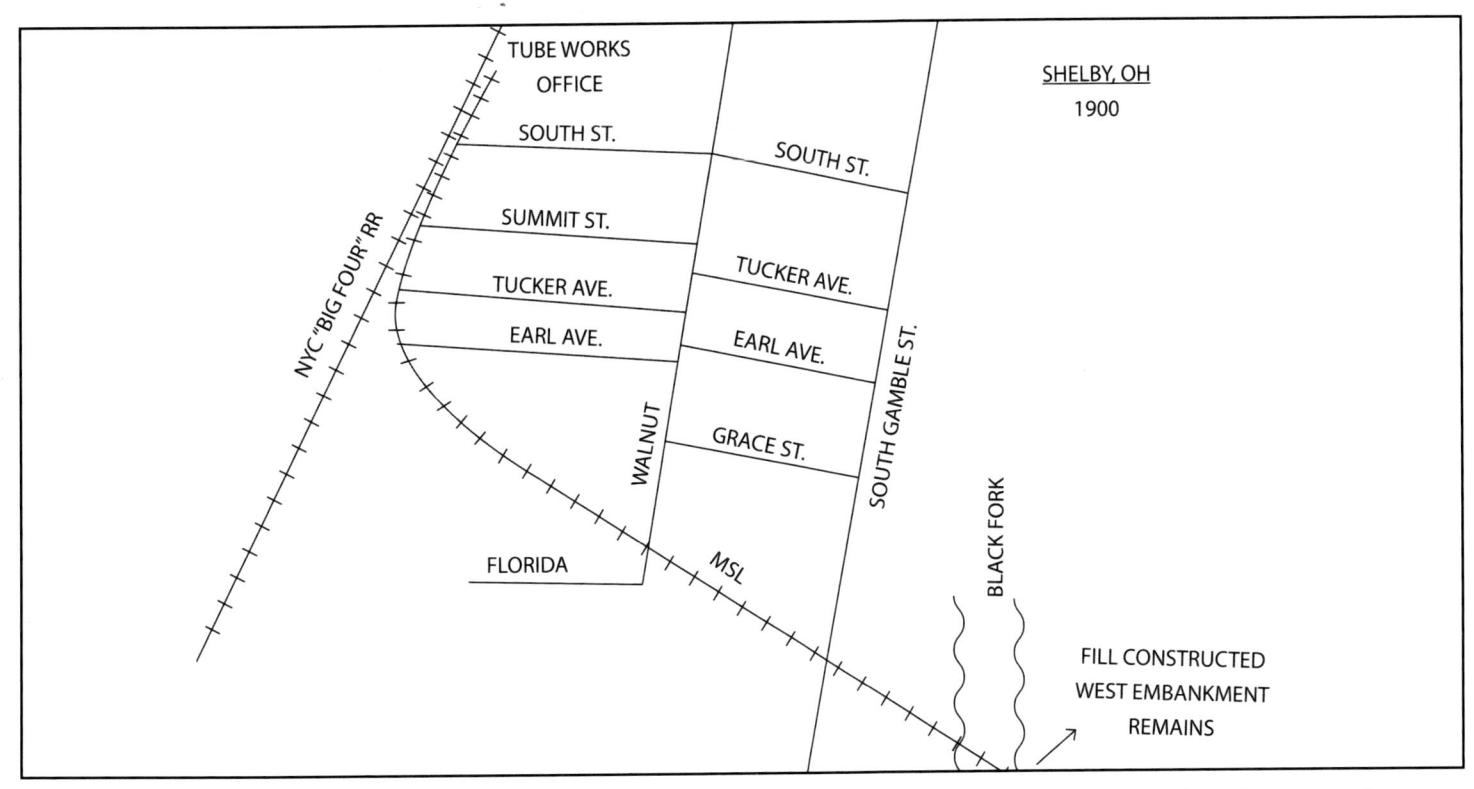

The MSL was actually constructed from Shelby to Mansfield. Work began at the old Tube Works Office north of South Street on the east side of the Big Four Railroad. Between the ends of Summit and Tucker the line began curving southeast and ran on a southeast tangent more or less to a point east of Leppo Road where it picked up the B&O. The ordinance called for an overpass over South Gamble Street. The west embankment at the Black Fork remains today.

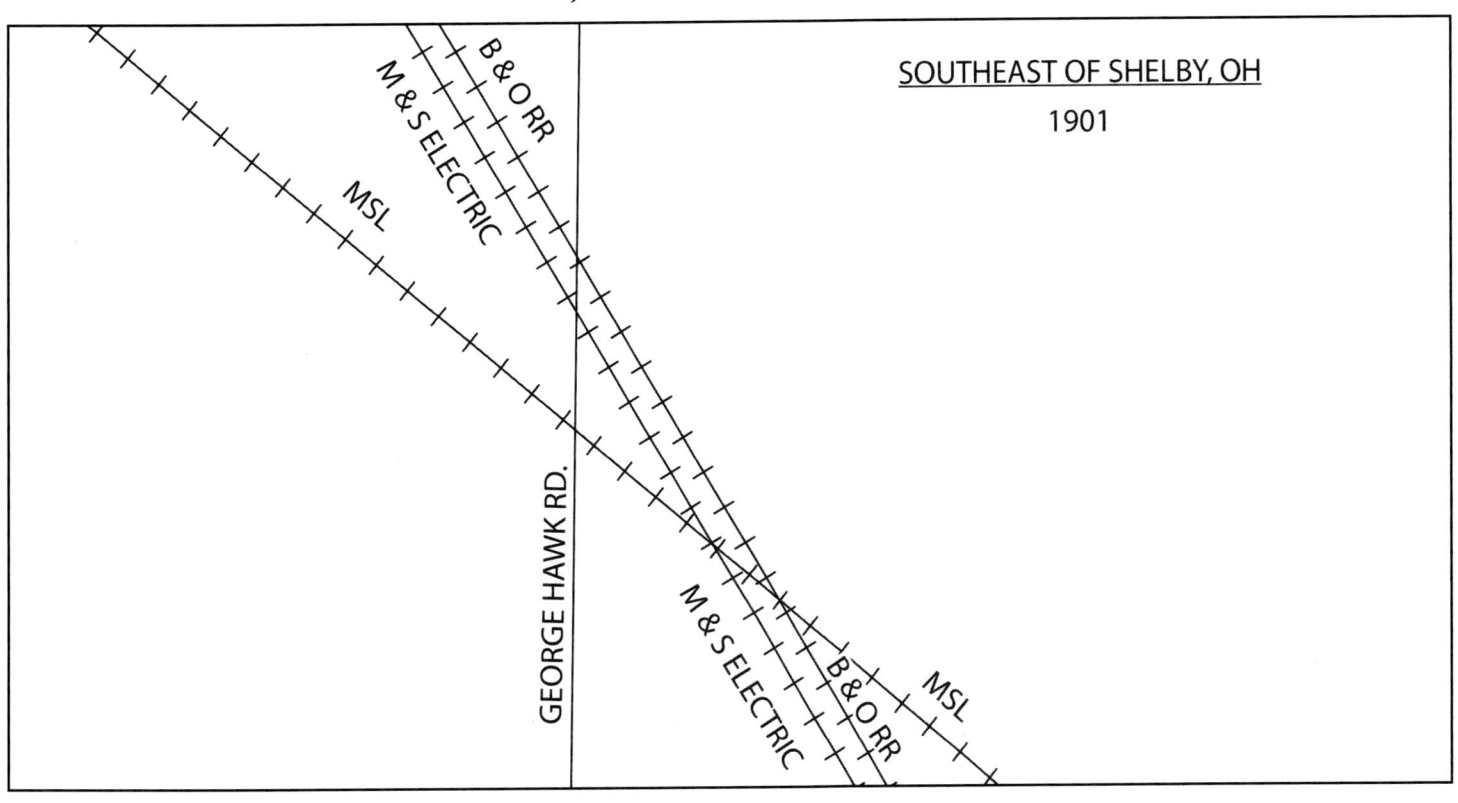

At George Hawk Road southeast of Shelby the MSL crossed the M&S interurban line and the B&O. This is the only place in the country that a paper railroad crossed both an interurban and a railroad line.

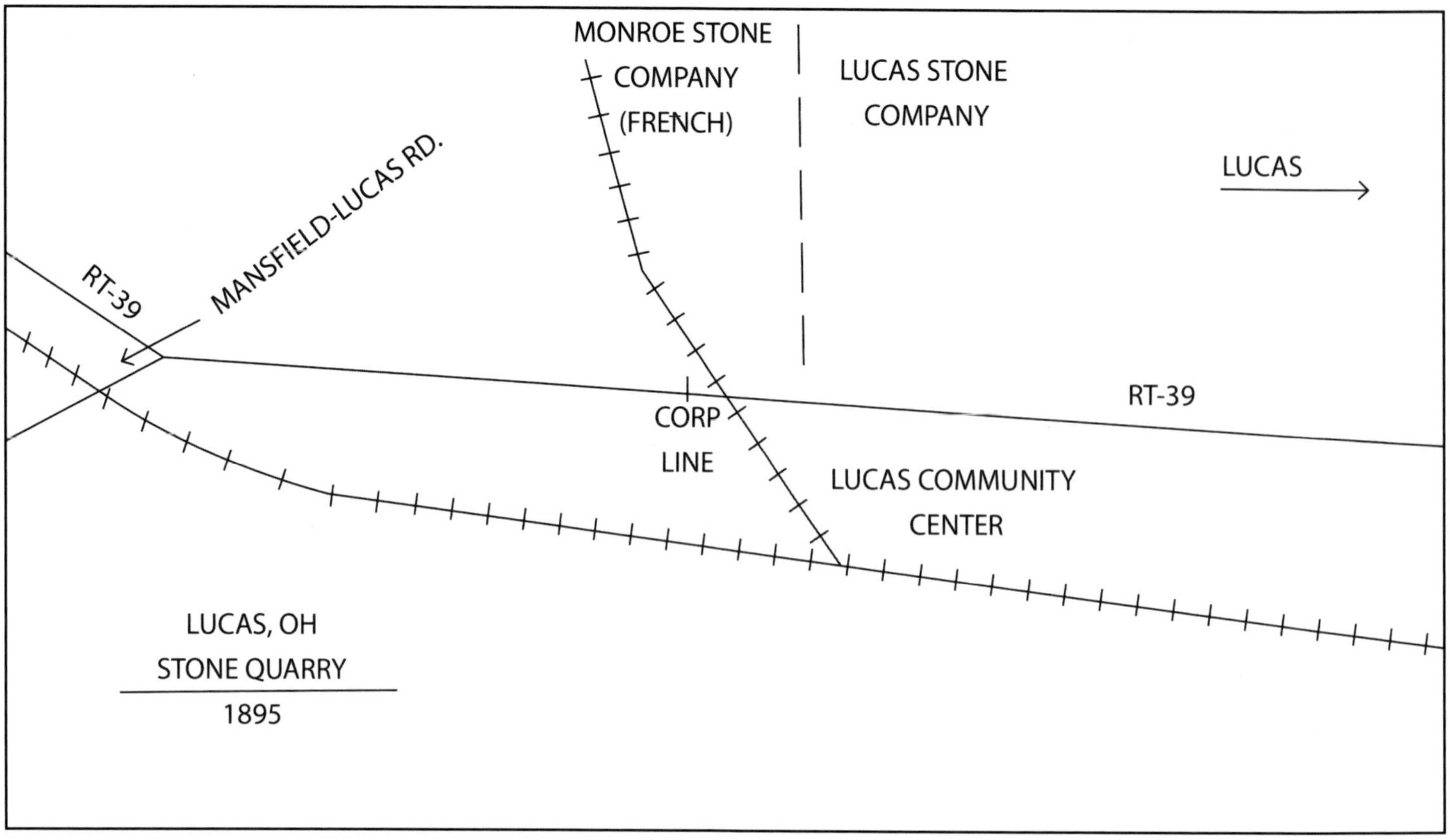
MONROE STONE
COMPANY
(FRENCH)
LUCAS STONE
COMPANY
LUCAS
MANSFIELD-LUCAS RD.
RT-39
CORP
LINE
RT-39
LUCAS COMMUNITY
CENTER
LUCAS, OH
STONE QUARRY
1895

The Northwest and Monroe Railroad Company operated in Lucas, OH from the Pennsylvania Railroad to the quarry and was a whopping ¼ - ½ mile long. It ran up the hill into the quarry after crossing Rt. 39 on the west edge of town as shown. The quarry as a whole stopped operations in 1898 when it was sold to T. A. Parry. The spur track was removed in October 1900.

ACKNOWLEDGMENTS

My Wife, Laurie: I have no idea how she had the patience to put up with me doing this research and putting this volume together. I'm sure while she was taking care of the children or doing house chores I irritated her greatly by obliviously typing away on my laptop. However, she always supported me in this endeavor and has always encouraged me to complete this.

My Father, Jim: This is an obvious acknowledgment. My father Jim is the one who sparked my interest in railroads, interurbans, and streetcars. As far back as I can remember, we were "out on the trail."

Dennis Lamont: I owe this entire project to Dennis. His interest and dedication studying the Sandusky, Norwalk, and Mansfield Electric Railway laid the entire foundation for the body of work completed so far. He also spent hours on end traveling to various historical societies and organizations collecting and scanning photos, which were contributed to this volume.

Bradley Knapp: Thank you Brad for the intense technical research you did in all facets of the book. I'm sure you will join me on many more explorations and it is much appreciated.

Tom Clabaugh: Tom deserves some sort of medal, trophy, or even cash for his efforts. I cannot thank Tom enough. He spent countless hours running around for me, finding and scanning photos. Oftentimes he'd leave his home after eating dinner to head down to the museum to look through folders of photos. If he found one he knew I'd like, sure enough it was scanned and emailed to me almost immediately.

Tim McKee: Tim spent many hours with me communicating via email on the topic. His generosity in donating photos to this project was vital to the success of this volume. Not only that, it was inspiring to see how he could make the history meaningful. Tim shared many high-resolution photos with me, and no doubt he will share more. The entire community owes Tim a heap of gratitude and I will never be able to truly repay him.

Alan Wigton: Alan is the president of the Richland County Historical Society. He invited me to speak in September of 2019 to the society on this very topic. Alan has really encouraged and pushed me to complete this. I worked with Alan to publish this on behalf of the RCHS.

Ed Sheridan: Ed spent many hours researching the Mansfield Short Line Railroad with me.

There are many, many others who contributed, names I cannot list, otherwise this book would be 1000 pages long. Thank you to all who helped!

JOIN ME!
Join me again in *Streetcars and Interurbans of Richland County, Ohio, Volume II: The Mansfield Streetcar System*. This second volume will explore in depth the history and photos of the streetcars that once ran in Mansfield.